CONVERSATIONS
with
GOD

*A YEAR OF PRAYER,
REFLECTION, AND
SPIRITUAL RENEWAL*

C P BEAUVOIR

Copyright © 2026 by C P Beauvoir

All rights reserved.

No part of this publication may be reproduced, distributed, or transmitted in any form or by any means, including photocopying, recording, or other electronic or mechanical methods, without the prior written permission from the publisher, except in the case of brief quotations embodied in critical reviews and certain other noncommercial uses permitted by copyright law.

ISBN: 978-0-9975066-8-6 (Hardcover)
ISBN: 978-0-9975066-9-3 (Paperback)
ISBN: 979-8-9941210-0-9 (E-book)
ISBN: 979-8-9941210-1-6 (Audiobook)

Printed in the United States of America

Written by C P Beauvoir
Published by Leef Publishing LLC
Cover Design and Formatting by Damonza

www.cpbeauvoir.com
www.leefpublishing.com

Contents

Introduction 1
January: New Beginnings 3
February: Love & Intimacy 36
March: Growth & Renewal 66
April: Presence & Stillness 98
May: Purpose & Identity 130
June: Joy & Celebration 163
July: Freedom & Courage 195
August: Trust & Faith 228
September: Wisdom & Discernment 261
October: Surrender & Healing 293
November: Gratitude & Reflection 326
December: Return to Worship 358
A Benediction For The Soul 392
A Note From The Author 393

also by C P Beauvoir

Guided Journal

Hi God, it's me

Poetry

things left unsaid
earth ignored your cries

for

God

You keep me
safe in all things

Introduction

This book is a quiet space.

A meeting place between your heart and God's. You don't have to come perfect, certain, or composed. You only have to come honest. Every page is a doorway to presence. A place to sit with God, to listen, to contemplate, to breathe, to remember that prayer isn't performance.

It's conversation. It's communion.

It's love speaking softly back and forth between you and the Divine.

You may enter these pages with questions. With longing. With joy. With ache. However you come is holy. God is not waiting for you to have the right words. He's waiting for you to bring your true ones. Let this be your sacred rhythm: to show up daily, to pour out freely, and to rest deeply in the knowing that your prayers are always heard.

God is listening. God is here.

He's always with you.

Each time you take a moment to pray, you nurture your conversations with God. This book is an invitation to abide in God's heart where you are always welcomed, always heard, always seen, always loved.

JANUARY

New Beginnings

There is a holiness in beginnings.

In the quiet space between what was and what will be, God leans near and whispers, "Start again with Me." Every sunrise is a reminder that grace still flows, that mercy still moves, that nothing is ever too late to be made new. The sacredness of beginning is not found in what you can plan or perfect, but in your willingness to pause, to listen, and to let God breathe His presence into what you're becoming.

This month is not about resolutions or reinvention.

It's about returning to stillness, to surrender, to the steady rhythm of His unfolding will. Here, you are invited to lay down the rush and the noise. You're invited to remember that beginnings are not born from effort but from openness. Every time you slow your pace to match God's, something eternal stirs.

Beginning again with God is not starting over.

It's starting deeper.

Beginnings rarely arrive as triumphs. Sometimes they come quietly, clothed in weariness or uncertainty. Yet even when your hands tremble, God is already holding them. The first step you take, hesitant and unsure, is already wrapped in His peace. God turns your uncertainty into invitation, your small *yes* into something holy.

God is the stillness beneath your striving, the grace within your waiting, the light that rises softly inside you. You don't have to know the way. You only have to open your heart to the One who walks beside you. When you do, even silence becomes prayer, and every breath becomes communion.

Before you turn these pages, breathe.

Let your soul remember that newness is not something you chase. It's something you receive. God is making all things new, even now, even here, even you. Let this be your beginning. Let this be your becoming.

Begin again with God, in truth, in light, in love.

January 1

Hi God, it's me.

It's a brand new year, and I want to say I'm hopeful; but the truth is, I'm simply weary.

Dear God, I know You're here,
even when I can't feel You near.

Still, my heart reaches for You
in the spaces where silence lingers.

Sweet, Loving God, don't let me drift too far.

When I pull away, draw me closer.

Hold me steady in the shelter of Your peace.

I need to rest in the gentleness of Your arms, to remember what safety feels like inside Your love.

I need the calm of Your divine presence.

The healing, the wholeness,
the quiet reminder that I belong to You.

My only prayer for this new year
is simple and sacred: *hold me close.*

Hold me, dear God, hold me.
Hold me and never let me go.

January 2

Hi God, it's me.

This morning feels different.

The world is quiet,
but my heart feels alive again.

Maybe this is what new beginnings sound like.
Not loud, not rushed, just steady and sacred.

I can feel You here, in the sunlight touching my window,
in the breath that fills my chest, in the simple grace of being.

You make all things new.

Not just around me, but within me.

You turn ordinary moments
into reminders of Your presence.

Thank You for the beauty of beginning again.

For the mercy that meets me every morning,
and the joy that hums softly beneath it all.

This day is a song of peace.

My life reflects Your goodness.

Every step I take
blooms with quiet joy,
for You are here.

January 3

Hi God, it's me.

Today feels like a whisper.

An invitation to grow without rushing.

I used to think becoming meant doing more.

But now, I see it's about letting
You shape me from the inside out.

You're teaching me transformation
doesn't always look like progress.

Sometimes, it looks like patience.
Sometimes, it sounds like silence.

Dear God, help me honor
the slow work of Your hands.

Remind me every unseen moment
is still sacred, still part of the making.

When I can't yet see the fruit, let me
trust the roots You're deepening in me.

When I feel small, remind me
even the smallest seeds carry promise.

You are forming something beautiful here.

I will not rush what is holy.

January 4

Hi God, it's me.

Today
I just want to thank You
for the gift of being here.

For the breath that moves through me.
For the sunlight that spills across my floor.

For the small,
quiet moments that whisper,
this is enough.

I don't need everything
to change to feel Your goodness.

It's already here, woven
into every second I'm alive.

You're in the pause before the prayer, in the laughter I didn't expect, in the peace that meets me when I finally stop searching.

God, teach me how to see You in the familiar.
To recognize holiness in the rhythm of today.

My heart delights
to the beauty around me,
and the beauty within me.

Beauty begins and ends with You.

January 5

Hi God, it's me.

Today I'm reminded
that faith is not fragile.

It's the certainty of knowing
You are who You say You are.

Even when I can't see the whole
picture, my spirit is sure of this:

You are faithful,
and every beginning You breathe
into being is already held in completion.

Dear God, help me rest in that certainty.

To trust that Your hand guides every step before I take it.
To remember that what feels small to me is seen fully by You.

You are the God who finishes what You start.

The One who turns unseen things
into miracles of timing and grace.

I walk forward in confidence.
Not because I know the way.

But because I know the One who goes before me.

January 6

Hi God, it's me.

Today feels bright,
like something within me
has quietly awakened.

Hope is stirring again.

Not as a wish or a dream.

But as a certainty rooted in Your goodness.

You remind me
every dawn carries promise,
every breath proves Your presence.

Dear God, thank You for the way You renew me.

For the joy that returns after long seasons of waiting.
For the peace that comes from trusting You completely.

You make all things new.

Not once.

But again and again.

And somehow, You make me new with them.

I rise today with quiet wonder, open hands, and a heart
ready to receive the miracles You've prepared to unfold.

January 7

Hi God, it's me.

I don't really have a list today.

I'm not even sure what I need.

I just want to be with You.

To sit in the quiet
and know that
You are near.

Sometimes, I think prayer
has to be loud, or long,
or emotional.

But maybe just being here is enough.

If You have something to say, I'm listening.

If not, I'll just stay close,
and breathe with You awhile.

Keep me close to You, dear God.

Give me a sacred home in the deepest parts of You.

January 8

Hi God, it's me.

Today,
I don't want
to speak first.

I just want to listen.

I want to hear the language of Your presence. The way
peace hums softly beneath the noise of the world.

So much around me
asks for my attention.

But only You hold my devotion.

Only You speak to what's eternal in me.

Dear God, teach me to recognize the sound of Your voice
in the pause before I respond, in the nudge toward kindness.

Teach me to hear You
in the thought that feels
like mercy arriving unannounced.

I don't want to rush through this day.
I want to move at the pace of Your Spirit.

To walk as one who hears, and in hearing—obeys.

My heart stays open quiet enough
for Heaven to have a home in me.

January 9

Hi God, it's me.

I'm beginning to see that every new
beginning requires a gentle release.

To step into what's next, I have
to loosen my hold on what was.

You can't fill hands that cling too tightly.

So I open mine; slowly, reverently,
trusting that surrender isn't an ending,
but the start of something holy.

Dear God, teach me to see
letting go as an act of becoming.

Teach me to trust what You remove
makes room for what is meant to grow.

Every time I yield, You breathe life into what's waiting.
Every time I release, You renew what I thought was gone.

Surrender and beginning
belong to each other.

They meet in Your presence, where endings turn to dawns;
where all creations learn again how to begin and end with You.

January 10

Hi God, it's me.

There's a stillness in me today.
Not empty, but full of peace.

Maybe this is how
new beginnings grow.

Not always in motion.

But in stillness
that trusts Your hands.

The waiting is not weakness.
It's where faith gathers strength.

Dear God, teach me
to rest in Your rhythm;
to pause without worrying,
and know silence is sacred.

Here, in the calm of Your presence, I become.

In this stillness, I am whole.

January 11

Hi God, it's me.

Peace feels like a whisper today. Soft but certain, settling gently over my soul.

It doesn't ask for proof or perfection.

It simply arrives.

A gift I could never earn.

Only receive.

Dear God, thank You for the kind of peace that doesn't depend on the circumstance.

Peace that stays even when life feels unsure.

Teach me to carry it like breath; quietly, faithfully, everywhere I go.

When the noise of the world grows loud, let Your peace speak louder.

When fear tries to rush in, let stillness answer first.

Dear God, You are my calm, my center, my steady ground.

In Your presence, I am home.

January 12

Hi God, it's me.

Peace has settled in, and
now I feel ready to move.

Not in haste, but in harmony with You.

Your light feels different now.

Not distant.

But near enough to follow.

It doesn't rush me.

It simply reveals the beauty of beginning again.

Dear God,
be the glow before my feet,
the warmth that keeps me steady.

When I can't see far ahead,
let me trust the light of You.

Every new beginning is born in Your guidance,
shaped by Your grace and sustained by Your love.

I walk forward,
one step, one light, one prayer at a time;
knowing where You lead, new life always begins.

January 13

Hi God, it's me.

I'm
learning obedience
isn't about control.

It's about trust.

Every new beginning asks for a *yes*.
A surrender of my way for Yours.

Your voice doesn't push.

It invites.

It leads gently toward what is good.

Dear God, teach me to follow without hesitation.
To see obedience not as a burden, but as belonging.

Each time I say *yes* to You,
something in me opens,
something in me grows.

Your will isn't confinement.

It's creation.

It's where my becoming begins.

January 14

Hi God, it's me.

Love feels different when it begins in You.
It's softer, truer, steady; even when life is not.

You've shown me
new beginnings
aren't just for me.

They're meant to pour through me.

My heart is a vessel of Your love;
kindness flows where impatience once lived.

Within my heart, compassion rises
where judgment used to stay.

Every time I love like You,
something in me is renewed.

Something in the world is, too.

You are the source.
I am the offering.

My life constantly reflects
the beauty of Your love.

January 15

Hi God, it's me.

I want to walk with You today.

Not ahead.
Not behind.

But here, in step with grace.

Each breath is a beginning.
Each moment, a quiet unfolding.

You are near in ways I can't explain.

Soft.
True.
Holy.

Dear God, when I drift, please lead me back gently.
Keep my heart open to where Your presence moves.

As I move through this day,
let my soul remember
I'm never alone.

All I need is You.

January 16

Hi God, it's me.

I used to search for purpose in what's ahead.
In the dreams, in the plans, in the someday.

You keep bringing me back here.

To the now.

To the breath that reminds
me I'm alive for a reason.

Dear God, teach me to see purpose
woven into the moments I often overlook.

The quiet tasks, the gentle pauses,
the way love moves through ordinary things.

You are here, and purpose is too.

It shimmers softly
beneath what seems
simple.

A quiet light guiding me home
to the meaning of what was never lost.

January 17

Hi God, it's me.

Thank You for the people
who remind me I'm not alone.

A text.
A hug.

A laugh that found me
when I needed it most.

I know
that was You showing up through them.
Loving me in ways I couldn't love myself.

God, bless the ones who showed up for me.
Cover them in peace, in grace, in perfect love.

Whisper
to their hearts
that they matter.

That their kindness is holy.

I see You in them, God.

In every gesture of care,
every moment of light.

Thank You for reminding me
that love is how You appear.

January 18

Hi God, it's me.

Some days, courage
looks like continuing.

Not running ahead.
Not giving up.

Just breathing and believing again.

You remind me
strength doesn't always roar.

Sometimes it's a whisper.
A single step taken in faith.

Dear God, when my heart grows tired, steady me.
When hope feels faint, breathe new life into me.

Remind me every step I take with You
is progress, even when it feels small.

Courage isn't the absence of fear.

It's the choice to keep
walking with You beside me.

Each step is something new being born.

January 19

Hi God, it's me.

I want to move with grace.

Not perfection.
Not pressure.

Just grace.

The kind
that lets me breathe, start again,
and soften where I once held tight.

Dear God, teach me to be
gentle with myself as I grow.

To honor
the parts of me still healing,
still learning, still becoming.

Let grace shape
the way I speak, the way I listen,
the way I move through the world.

Dear God, when I stumble,
remind me that every beginning
has room for compassion, room to rise,
room to return, room to begin again with You.

January 20

Hi God, it's me.

Thank You for reminding me
that love doesn't end with me.

Sometimes,
the new beginning
You're shaping in my heart
is meant to reach someone else's.

Dear God, if there is someone
who needs comfort, let me carry it softly.

If someone needs kindness, let my words be warm.
If someone needs light, let my presence reflect Yours.

I don't need to know
who or where or how.

Just make me available.

Dear God,
I'm open, willing, and ready to
respond to Your gentle leading.

Use my life as a quiet answer
to a prayer I may never hear.

January 21

Hi God, it's me.

I don't even know
what to pray for today.

There's so much swirling inside me.

But You know, don't You?

Before I think.
Before I speak.
Before I act.

You know all of me.

Dear God,
thank You for understanding me
better than I understand myself.

Thank You for sitting
with me in the silence.

I don't need to say much today.
I just need to be here with You.

January 22

Hi God, it's me.

I want to be still.

To stop striving.
To stop performing.

I don't want to impress You.

I want to honor You.

God, can we simply sit together?

No expectations.
No to-do list.

Just presence.
Just peace.

I feel safest when I'm with You.

January 23

Hi God, it's me.

I almost gave up today.
Almost let the weight win.

But out of nowhere
You reminded me
to keep going.

You're with me.

And with You,
I'm never alone.

Dear God,
thank You for strength
I didn't know I had.

And for hope that rises even in the dark,
whispering that every moment can become
a new beginning when I turn toward You.

Keep me close to You, Sweet, Loving God.

I don't want to do this without You.

Dear God, You complete me.

January 24

Hi God, it's me.

Today feels bright, like the air
itself is opening a little wider.

There's a softness in me.
A quiet joy I didn't have to chase.

You're lifting me, lightening me,
reminding me that new beginnings
carry their own kind of happiness.

Dear God, thank You for the
peace that feels like sunshine.

Thank You for the joy that rises
without warning, gentle but full.

You start things in me with such kindness.
Little sparks of hope, small bursts of clarity.
Moments that feel like fresh grace unfolding.

Every time I lean into You,
something good awakens.

Something alive.
Something new.

Stay close to me, God.

There's joy in beginning again with You.

January 25

Hi God, it's me.

As this month begins to settle, I feel
something tender awakening in me.

A deeper closeness.

A quiet knowing that beginning
again is not just an invitation.

It's a journey with You.

I can sense You drawing me into the year ahead
with a gentleness that asks nothing but my heart.

Dear God, teach me to honor
the beginnings You place before me.

Not with pressure.
But with presence.

Help me step into this new year with open hands, soft
expectations, and a spirit willing to be shaped by Your love.

There's something sacred about starting again with You.
It's like returning home to a place my soul never truly left.

Stay close, God.

Walk with me into all I'm becoming.

January 26

Hi God, it's me.

I've been thinking about the year ahead.

Not with worry.
Not with striving.

But
with a soft openness
I didn't have before.

Beginning again feels different this time.

It feels quieter.
More intentional.

More like something You and I are doing together.

Dear God, show me how to enter this year with
a heart that listens more than it demands,
a mind that trusts more than it fears.

I don't need to see the whole path.

I just need to know You're in each step,
guiding, revealing, shaping what's meant to be.

If this year becomes anything at all,
let it become a deeper walk with You.

January 27

Hi God, it's me.

Something quiet is opening in me.

A soft settling.

A deep breath I didn't know I needed.

This beginning no longer feels like a moment.

But a becoming.

A slow unfolding of who I am with You.

Dear God,
hold my heart steady
as I step into what's ahead.

Your presence is the rhythm of my days.

The whisper that reminds me I'm being
made new in ways that only Heaven sees.

Stay with me, dear God.

I'm listening.
I'm yielding.

I'm beginning again with You.

January 28

Hi God, it's me.

I felt You today.

Not in a rush of emotions, but in
a calm that settled deep inside me.

A quiet reminder You're here
before I even call Your name.

I sensed You
in the stillness of my thoughts,
in the warmth of a moment,
in the ease of simply breathing.

Thank You for meeting me in the gentle things.

In the peace that softens me, in the presence that steadies
me, in the love that keeps unfolding throughout the day.

Dear God, help me stay aware of You.

The God who moves softly, speaks tenderly,
and holds me even when I don't notice.

My heart recognizes You again and again.

I see You.

January 29

Hi God, it's me.

As this month nears its end, I find myself looking
back at all the ways You've met me in the quiet.

In the small moments.
In the gentle shifts.

In the breaths that carried
more peace than I expected.

Dear God, thank You for shaping me in ways I didn't always see.
Thank You for touching places in my heart that needed softening.

Thank You, Father,
for beginning things in me
that only You could begin.

You've been near:

in every step, every whisper, every still place
where my soul paused long enough to feel You.

As I move toward the end of the month,
keep my spirit attentive and my heart open.

Keep my eyes trained on the subtle ways
You reveal Yourself again and again.

I want to finish this month
inhaling You in every breath.

January 30

Hi God, it's me.

There's a tenderness in my spirit today.

A gentle awareness of how You've walked
with me through every moment of this month.

Not loudly.
Not dramatically.

But faithfully.

Quietly.
Constantly.

Dear God, thank You
for being the One who stayed close
even when I wasn't paying attention.

Peace has settled over me in ways I can't explain.
Clarity came soft and gentle, one breath at a time.

I can feel You making space in me.

Space for newness, space for hope,
space for whatever You're shaping next.

Keep me open, dear God.
Keep me aware. Keep me steady.

Keep me close as I continue to begin again with You.

January 31

Hi God, it's me.

We've reached the end of this month.

My heart feels full in a way
I can't quite put into words.

You've met me in stillness, in surrender, in the smallest
moments that became holy because You were there.

Thank You for every new beginning
You've planted in me this month.

The healing that started quietly
and the faith that grew deeper.

Dear God, thank You
for the closeness that wrapped itself
around my days like a soft light.

As I step into a new month, I don't ask for certainty.

I ask for You.

Stay near.
Stay gentle.
Stay loving.

Stay at the center of everything I become.

With You, dear God, every ending
is only the start of something new.

FEBRUARY

Love & Intimacy

Love is the language of God.

It's how He speaks, how He moves, how He reaches for you in every quiet moment. This month, you are invited to remember you're already loved; fully, freely, and without conditions. There's nothing to earn. Nothing to prove. Just a love that holds you even when you turn away, a love that stays when everything else fades.

God's love isn't distant or reserved.

It's near. It's tender.

It shows up in the stillness when no one else sees. It meets you in your longing and calls you by name. This love is not performance. It's presence. It doesn't demand that you be perfect. Only that you be willing to receive what has always been yours.

Let this be the month you soften. The month you let love find you in the mirror, in the silence, in every heartbeat that reminds you that you're alive for a reason. God loves you always and forever; throughout eternity and beyond.

Love is not something you chase. It's something you return to. It's your heritage. It's your legacy. God's love is your birthright. It teaches you how to forgive, how to release, how to rest. Love begins with God, flows through you, and touches everything you do. This is the sacred intimacy of February. Come home to love.

February 1

Hi God, it's me.

I've been thinking
a lot about love lately.

What it means. How it feels.
Why sometimes, it hurts so much?

But then, I remember You, Sweet, Loving God.

How You love me without conditions.
Without holding my flaws against me.
Without keeping score.

It's hard for me to understand that kind of love.

I've been taught I have to earn it.

Perform for it.
Deserve it.

You love me just as I am.

Even when I question it.
Even when I pull away.

Sweet, Loving God, wrap me in Your love always.

Not because I've done anything right.

But because You always do.

February 2

Hi God, it's me.

Thank You for the way You slip into
my day so gently I almost miss it.

A kind word.

A warm light through the window. A breath
that suddenly softens for reasons I can't explain.

These small mercies are Your hands
writing little love notes for my spirit.

Sometimes, I wait for the skies to open for something big
and undeniable. And all along, You've been loving me quietly.

Faithfully.

Sweet, Loving God,
teach my heart to notice You.

To pause.
To pay attention.

To honor the tiny miracles
that carry me through the day.

You are with me, God; in the hush, in the
stillness, in the beauty I rarely slow down to see.

And for every gentle way You love me
back to life, I will always love You.

February 3

Hi God, it's me.

I love how You remind me how softly You move.
How faithfully You show up in the small corners of my life.

I've been
trying so hard to earn
what You already gave me.

Trying to perfect myself. Trying to prove I'm worthy. Trying to "measure up" to a version of me that feels forever out of reach.

But You're not asking for that.
You're asking for me as I am.

Here and now.

With my flaws. With my effort. With my heart
that's learning how to trust softness again.

Thank You for loving me before I change,
before I improve, before I understand.

Your love is not an earthly reward.

It's a holy presence.

Teach me to rest in that, breathe in that;
to know I'm held even when I'm still growing.

God, help me receive the gentle way You love me.

February 4

Hi God, it's me.

Can You please help
me love like You do?

Sometimes,
loving people
feels like work.

When I feel taken for granted.

When I'm misunderstood
and want to walk away.

You don't walk away.

Not from me.
Not ever.

Dear God, please teach me how to stay tender.

Teach me how to choose kindness when I'm hurting.
Teach me how to forgive when it seems impossible.

I don't want to love like the world does.

I want to love like You.

February 5

Hi God, it's me.

There are some hurts I haven't let go of.

Not because I want to keep them.
But because I don't know how.

I carry them like protection.

Like if I hold them long enough,
they'll hurt less someday.

But they don't.

They just make it harder to breathe.

Dear God, can You please
show me how to forgive?

Not just others.
But myself too.

I want to live light again.

I want peace more than I want to be right.

Please help me heal.

Dear God, I'm ready.

February 6

Hi God, it's me.

Thank You for showing up through people.

In laughter. In kindness.

In quiet support
that doesn't ask
for anything back.

You keep sending me love
through the ones who know You.

Sometimes, even through the ones who don't.

Dear God,
please help me see
these moments as sacred.

Not random.
Not luck.

But love on purpose.

Let me be that for someone else too.

Let my heart extend Your grace.
Let my life echo Your goodness.

Let me be a reflection of the love that is You.

February 7

Hi God, it's me.

I want to love myself.

Not just tolerate myself.
Not just manage my flaws.

But love the person You made.

I don't want
to pick myself
apart today.

I want to see what You see.

Someone worthy.

Beautiful.
True.

Held together by grace.

Dear God, please teach me how to be kinder inside.
To speak gently to the parts of me that are still healing.

You didn't make a mistake when You made me.

Help me believe that.

Sweet, Loving God,
help me see myself
the way You see me.

February 8

Hi God, it's me.

I've been
feeling unsure about everything.
About what's next. About myself.

Uncertainty wraps around me like fog.

No matter how hard I try to see
ahead, nothing becomes clear.

But even here, in this blurriness, I feel Your nearness.

Your love touches the edges of my fear.

Your presence rests against my heart like something steady.

Something intimate.
Something safe.

I don't know where I'm going.
I don't know what's unfolding.

So please, dear God, please take my hand.

Hold it close.

Walk with me through this.
I don't need the destination.

I just need You near me, loving me and guiding me.

February 9

Hi God, it's me.

Yesterday, I asked You to take my hand.
Today, I feel You closer than I expected.

Not loud.
Not dramatic.

Just a warmth in my chest,
a quiet knowing that You're near.

There's a tenderness in the way You stay with me.

Even when I'm tired.
Even when I'm unsure.
Even when I feel hard to hold.

You don't pull away.
You draw nearer.

God, teach me to rest in this closeness with You.

Teach me to lean in, to breathe with You,
to trust the rhythm of being loved so gently.

I don't have all the answers.
But I have Your presence.

The tender place where my soul meets Yours.

February 10

Hi God, it's me.

There's a holiness
in the way You hold me.

Quiet. Unforced. Near.

You don't rush my heart.
You don't demand clarity.

You simply stay until my spirit
remembers it's safe to breathe again.

You see the thoughts I never speak, the longing
beneath the silence, the ache I try to carry alone.

And somehow, in Your presence, none of it feels too heavy.

Sweet, Loving God, thank You for meeting me in the hidden
places. For touching the parts of me I keep tucked away.

Thank You for loving me gently enough,
that nothing feels unworthy in Your hands.

Draw me closer today, dear God.

Teach me the intimacy of being
fully known and never turned away.

With You, I am held.
With You, I am home.

February 11

Hi God, it's me.

There's something
tender about waking up
and knowing You're already here.

Before I speak.
Before I think.

Before I gather myself back into strength.

Your presence waits for me like morning light,
soft enough not to startle me, steady enough to hold me.

Sometimes, I wonder how You can love me with such gentleness.

How You stay close even when my heart feels distant.
How You reach for me even when I run far from You.

But this is who You are.

The God who lingers, the God who stays,
the God who loves without hesitation.

Dear God, teach me how to lean into this holy nearness.
Teach me to open my hands, my worries, my guarded places.

Your love fills where I'm empty.
Your peace heals where I'm hurting.

Being close to You is the most intimate truth I know.
And today, I choose to rest in the God who never leaves.

February 12

Hi God, it's me.

There's a quiet place inside
me that only You can reach.

A place even I forget about.
A place I avoid when life feels loud.
A place that softens only when You speak.

I felt it today.

That gentle stirring. That small opening in my spirit
where Your love slips in like light through a doorway.

You never force it.
You never rush it.

You just arrive, patient and faithful, until
the walls I built start to loosen in Your presence.

God, thank You for knowing how to touch my heart without
breaking it; for knowing how to enter the deepest parts
of me with tenderness, with patience, with holiness.

Teach me to welcome You there. Teach me
to open that quiet place a little more each day.

Where love becomes truth. Where fear was
never real. Where You and I meet in stillness.

Sweet, Loving God, that's intimacy to me.
The place where Your breath reaches mine.

February 13

Hi God, it's me.

I delight in the quiet way Your love
reaches for me before I even turn to You.

A soft pull in my spirit.
A gentle nudge in my breathing.

A holiness that enters
the room without sound.

You are the One
who seeks my heart
long before I realize I'm drifting.

Dear God, thank You for this sacred pursuit.

For finding me in hidden places. For calling me
back to stillness with nothing but Your presence.

I'm learning intimacy with
You is not something I earn.

It's something You offer again
and again with endless tenderness.

You always
find me first,
God of my heart.

And in that holy reaching,
I learn what intimacy truly is.

February 14

Hi God, it's me.

On a day when the world celebrates love,
my heart turns to You—the One who loved me first.

The One who loves me most. The One whose love
does not waver with mood or falter with time.

Your love is steady.

Ancient.
Ever-present.

A sanctuary my spirit returns to without needing permission.

God, thank You for loving me in ways no human language can
fully hold. Thank You for seeing every corner of me and staying.

You chose me long before I knew how to choose You.

I offer You the quiet chambers of my heart; the tender places,
the guarded places, the places still learning how to be loved well.

Dear God, wrap me in the kind of love that makes me whole.
Your presence is my closest companion, my truest intimacy.

No love is more faithful than Yours.
No love is more home than You.

Sweet, Loving God, on this day of love,
I rest in the One who has always loved me best.

February 15

Hi God, it's me.

Today my heart feels quiet.

Not heavy.
Not light.

Just open.

There's a softness in me that I know comes from You.
A tenderness that settles when I stop trying to carry myself.

Your love meets me here, in the in-between, in the
place where I'm simply human and simply Yours.

Dear God,
thank You for the intimacy
of being held without striving.

I don't need fireworks to feel close to You.

Just honesty.
Just breath.

Just the willingness to sit in Your presence.

Stay near me today.

Your love shapes my thoughts and steadies my spirit.
Dear God, make room inside me for peace to grow.

February 16

Hi God, it's me.

I feel something shifting
quietly inside me today.

A softness I didn't create.

A
peace
I couldn't have
made on my own.

It feels like You.

The way You move without force.
The way You heal without noise.

The way You reach the deepest
parts of me with nothing but love.

Dear God, thank You for tending to the hidden places. For shaping me gently and teaching my heart how to open again.

Your love is the quiet transformation growing inside me.

The gentle renewal making my heart new.

February 17

Hi God, it's me.

Today Your love felt like
an awakening in my spirit.

A stirring, a warmth, a gentle rising
of something I can't quite name.

It wasn't quiet this time.

It was alive.
It was moving.

It was calling something deep in me
to come forward and breathe again.

Intimacy is the way You awaken my soul.
How You touch places that have been sleeping.
How You revive what I thought was lost or forgotten.

Dear God, thank You for loving me
in ways that bring me back to life.

For lighting a fire where I had grown dim.
For reminding me that love is not only soft.

Sometimes it's a holy rising, a sacred pulse,
a divine echo that makes my whole heart respond.

Your love awakens me, God of my soul.

I'm grateful to be alive in You.

February 18

Hi God, it's me.

I'm learning trust
is a kind of love too.

A sacred tenderness,
a holy surrender of what I cannot see
into the hands of the One who sees everything.

Trust feels like opening when I would rather guard.
It feels like releasing when I want to hold tight.

It's choosing You especially when
I don't understand what You're doing.

Dear God,
teach my heart
to trust the way it loves:

fully, honestly, without hesitation.

You've never failed me. You've never abandoned me.
You have never withheld what was meant to bless me.

I place my uncertainties in Your hands
as an act of love, of devotion, and of faith.

Trusting You,
Sweet, Loving God,
is my way of saying,
Your love will carry me.

February 19

Hi God, it's me.

Today my heart feels drawn
into a deeper kind of love.

Not emotion.
Not desire.

But devotion.

A love that steadies my spirit.

A love that chooses You again and again because
my soul recognizes there is nowhere truer to turn.

Devotion is aligning my heart with Yours.

Not out of duty.
But out of reverence.

You are worthy. You are holy.
Loving You is breathing truth.

Dear God,
teach me to love You with a devotion
that is quiet, faithful, and unwavering.

My thoughts honor You. My choices reflect You. My life is
a small offering of love placed into Your beautiful hands.

You are my center. My steady place. My eternal devotion.

February 20

Hi God, it's me.

Today, I'm learning love is not
only what I give, but what I release.

Surrender is its own kind of love.

A holy yielding, a sacred unclenching
of everything I tried to control out of fear.

There's tenderness in placing my plans in Your hands.
There's trust in loosening the grip that keeps my heart tense.

There's intimacy in letting You
lead me where I cannot lead myself.

God, teach me the beauty of surrendered love.

The love that opens instead of resists.
The love that yields instead of grasps.

The love that trusts Your wisdom more than mine.

I give You my worries, my timing, my need to understand.

Not because I'm giving up, but because I'm giving in
to the One whose love has never failed me.

Surrender is my *yes* to You.

My quiet proof that You are good.

February 21

Hi God, it's me.

Today, I feel the grace of the divine feminine in me.

The softness, the intuition, the quiet strength
that rises without noise and loves without fear.

There's holiness in this part of me.

A sacred gentleness.

A wisdom that listens deeply
and feels the world with tenderness.

Sometimes, I forget that this too is made in Your image.

The nurturing, the sensing, the presence, the flowing
essence that reflects the beauty of Your own heart.

Dear God, thank You
for the divine feminine
You breathe into my spirit.

Teach me to trust the intuition that's also truth.
Teach me to honor the softness that's also strength.
Teach me to embrace the gentleness that's also power.

Your love awakens
the divine feminine in me;
whole, holy, beloved.

And today, I stand in that beauty with reverence.

February 22

Hi God, it's me.

Today, I feel the strength of the divine masculine in me.

The courage, the clarity, the steady presence that stands firm without force and protects without fear.

There's holiness in this part of me.

A sacred groundedness.

A wisdom that leads with integrity and moves through the world with quiet confidence.

Sometimes, I forget that this too is made in Your image.

The bravery, the discipline, the rootedness, the unwavering truth that reflects the steadfast strength of Your own heart.

Dear God, thank You
for the divine masculine
You breathe into my spirit.

Teach me to trust the boldness that's also wisdom.
Teach me to honor the strength that's also tenderness.
Teach me to embrace the power that's also humility.

Your love awakens
the divine masculine in me;
anchored, steady, beloved.

And today, I stand in that strength with reverence.

February 23

Hi God, it's me.

Your love reached places
in me I barely acknowledge.

The tender parts, the quiet aches,
the wounds I learned to carry.

You don't force healing on me.

You meet me softly.

You sit with what hurts
until the hurt begins to loosen.

Your love knows how to restore
what I thought would always ache.

It knows how to breathe warmth
into the cold corners of my heart.

Dear God,
thank You for mending me gently. For lifting what feels heavy.
For touching what I hide with kindness instead of judgment.

Teach me to open to the healing You offer. Teach me
to trust the slow, sacred work You're doing in me.

Your love is my restoration.
Today, I welcome its touch.

February 24

Hi God, it's me.

Today I felt something settle in me.
A quiet knowing that I belong to You.

Not because of what I do.
Not because I always get it right.

But because Your love claims
me in ways nothing else ever has.

There is a safety in You that
my soul keeps returning to.

A home I don't have to earn,
where I'm kept safe and warm.

Dear God, thank You
for giving me a belonging that cannot be shaken.
For choosing me before I learned to choose You.

Thank You for welcoming every part of me.
The sure, the unsure, the strong, the trembling.

Teach me to rest in this truth You keep offering.

I am Yours.

Fully.
Forever.

My heart is glad to come home to the One it belongs to.

February 25

Hi God, it's me.

Your love is the truest
thing I will ever know.

Not my fears.
Not my doubts.

Not
the stories I tell myself
when I feel unworthy.

Your love cuts through all of that.

Clear, steady, unwavering;
always reminding me who I am
and who I've always been to You.

You anchor me when my thoughts drift into shadows.
You speak truth where my insecurities whisper lies.
You bring clarity to the places I twist with worry.

Dear God, thank You for being
the truth my heart can trust.

Teach me to listen to the voice of love more than the voice of fear. To lean into what You say about me above everything else.

Your love is the truth that brings me back to myself.

February 26

Hi God, it's me.

Today I felt Your love
gathering the pieces of me.

The tired ones, the forgotten ones,
the ones I thought would never
feel whole again.

You restore me in ways
I barely notice at first.

A softened thought here. A lifted weight there.
A breath that feels easier than the one before.

Restoration with You is not sudden.

It's steady.

It's
quiet renewal woven into my days
until my heart begins to rise again.

God, thank You for making me whole
in places I didn't know were broken.

Teach me to trust the slow rebuilding, and to
welcome the new strength You're forming in me.

Your love restores what life has worn down.
Today, I open myself to being made new.

February 27

Hi God, it's me.

Your love opened something in me.

A clarity, a shimmer of understanding,
a truth rising gently to the surface of my spirit.

You reveal things not to overwhelm me.

But to free me.

To help me see
what I could not
name on my own.

Sometimes, the revelation is soft.

A gentle nudge, a shifting thought,
a moment that suddenly feels lit from within.

Other times, it's deeper.

A recognition of who I am, who You are, and
what Your love has been shaping in me all along.

Your love is revelation.

I open my spirit to the truth You unveil.

February 28

Hi God, it's me.

I'm noticing how Your love
doesn't just hold me.

It shapes me.

Slowly. Quietly. Gently.

I'm not who I was
at the start of this month.

Something in me is softer now.

Clearer now.

More open to You than I knew how to be before.

Your love changes me without forcing me. It grows me
without rushing me. It teaches me without shaming me.

Thank You for the becoming You are guiding within me.

The unfolding of my spirit, the deepening of my heart,
the quiet transformation that only love can create.

Dear God, teach me to welcome every shift, every
opening, every part of me that rises toward You.

Your love is making me into
who I was always meant to be.

I say *yes* to the becoming.

February 29

Hi God, it's me.

This day doesn't always come.

It's a day that feels borrowed. A day
that reminds me how precious time is.

And still, Your love moves
through it as faithfully as ever.

It doesn't wait for calendars.
It doesn't pause for seasons.
It doesn't shift with years.

Your love is steady.

Endless. Eternal.

Dear God, thank You for a love that outlives every moment.

Your love meets me in the ordinary and the rare, in the days
that come often and the ones that arrive only once in a while.

I anchor myself in what never changes.

Your presence. Your promise.
Your devotion to my heart.

On this extra day, I offer
all of me to You once again.

Your love is my eternity.

MARCH

Growth & Renewal

Growth is God's quiet miracle.

It rarely announces itself, yet it moves through every corner of your becoming. This month is not about perfection. It's about participation. About letting God do His deep work within you, even when it feels slow, unseen, or uncertain.

Growth begins where surrender takes root. There will be moments of stretching, of pruning, of letting go. None of it is wasted.

God removes what cannot stay, not to punish you, but to prepare you. Renewal happens when you stop resisting what He's reshaping and when you trust that the same hands that hold the seed will also bring the bloom. You don't have to rush the process. You don't have to understand it. You only have to stay open, to let the light in, to keep showing up in faith, to believe that something beautiful is forming in the dark.

So breathe through the tension. Lean into the becoming. Let this month remind you that transformation doesn't always look graceful. But it is holy. Every breaking, every blooming, every beginning is evidence that God is still at work in you. This is the season of renewal.

Grow gently. Grow with God.

March 1

Hi God, it's me.

A new month.
A new page.
A new me.

There's a quiet part of me
hoping something will shift.

I want to grow, God.

Not in ways people can see.
But in ways only You can.

Grow my patience. Grow my faith. Grow my love.
Grow the parts of me that don't bloom easily.

I don't want to rush the process.

I want to be open to it.
I want to trust it.

Whatever
You're doing in me,
please let it take root.

I give You the soil of my heart.

Plant what You will.

I trust You.

March 2

Hi God, it's me.

I've been craving change and
fearing it at the same time.

I say I want new things.

But sometimes, I cling to the
old because at least it's familiar.

You didn't call me to comfort.

You called me to grow.

So stretch me, God.

Challenge me.
Lead me.

When I get scared,
please remind me
who's holding my hand.

You're leading me
somewhere beautiful.

Thank You, God, for being patient
with me as I learn to trust Your way.

Take my fears, steady my steps, and guide
me into the life You've been preparing for me.

March 3

Hi God, it's me.

Today I noticed
something small.

Flowers blooming where before
I thought nothing could grow.

It made me think of You.

Of how You create
beauty in the cracks.

In the places that feel
forgotten and unseeing.

In the parts of me I thought
were too broken to matter.

God, thank You for not giving up on me.

Thank You for growing something in me
even when I didn't believe it was possible.

Dear God,
please help me
see what You see.

Help me water what You've planted.

I'm ready to bloom with You.

March 4

Hi God, it's me.

I've been feeling impatient.
I've been seeking answers.

Wishing everything
would happen faster.

You don't move on my timeline.
And maybe that's a good thing.

Still, it's hard to wait.

It's hard to trust
when I can't see
what You're doing.

Dear God, please teach me
how to rest in the waiting and
how to hope without hurrying.

God, show me how to sit still and know and
trust You're still working behind the scenes.

When I feel delayed, dear God,
remind me that You are never late.

You've proven it countless times over and over.
You are always on time each and every time.

Your timing is always perfect.

March 5

Hi God, it's me.

I've been holding on to old weight.
Things I told myself I already let go of.

I can still feel them
in the way I fight to protect myself
and in the way I hesitate to hope again.

Dear God,
can You please help me
release them for real?

The resentments.
The grudges.
The fears.

The memories that still
sting when I touch them.

I don't want to carry dead
things into living seasons.

I want to be free, God.

Free to be.

Light.
New.

Free with You.

March 6

Hi God, it's me.

I'm
starting to notice
small changes.

The way my thoughts are clearer.
The way I pause before immediately reacting.
The way I show myself just a little more grace.

That's You, isn't it?

Working quietly.

Transforming me gently.

I want to celebrate that today.

I want
to rejoice in the
progress no one sees.

The growth that
doesn't need
applause.

Dear God,
thank You for being patient
as I become more of You.

March 7

Hi God, it's me.

Growth isn't always graceful.

Some days, it's falling apart.

It's letting go
of everything
I used to rely on.

But if it's You tearing down the old,
then I trust what You're building
even when it's uncomfortable.

Dear God,
when everything hurts,
help me lean in, not away.

Help me believe pain has purpose.

I want to be rooted in You.

Strong.
Steady.

Still reaching for light.

Dear God, grow me
into something
You love.

March 8

Hi God, it's me.

I've been feeling weak lately.

In my body.
In my mind.
In my spirit.

In the way
I keep showing up
even when I feel empty.

I don't like admitting that.

But You already know, don't You?

I need strength today.

Not just to get through.

But to keep believing I can heal.

Yes, I can.

I can grow.
I can become.
I can transform.

Your strength is made perfect in my weakness.
So here I am, dear God, weak and willing.

Be my strength.

March 9

Hi God, it's me.

Trust
doesn't come
naturally to me.

I like to think ahead.

Prepare.
Plan.

Protect myself from disappointment.

You keep inviting me to let go.

To trust You
with the things
I can't understand
and can't control.

I want to say *yes*.

Even when my voice shakes.
Even when my heart hesitates.

God, please teach me how to let go.

Only when I let go can I trust You
fully, completely, and honestly.

Dear God, I am Yours.

March 10

Hi God, it's me.

I feel drained.

Not just physically
but emotionally.

Spiritually.

I feel drained deep down
where no one else sees.

I keep pouring out.

But I haven't been filled in a while.

Dear God,
can You please
pour into me today?

With peace.
With rest.

With
the kind of comfort
only You can give.

I don't want to keep running on empty.

Fill me, dear God.

I need You.

March 11

Hi God, it's me.

Some days
feel like repetition.

Same prayers.
Same battles.

Same questions
with no clear answers.

Still, You meet me every time.

Without frustration.
Without judgment.
Without shame.

Thank You for being the God
who doesn't get tired of my voice.

You never grow impatient
with my lifelong process.

Even when I feel stuck,
You stay close to me.

That means more than I can say.

Oh!
Faithful God,
I love You!

March 12

Hi God, it's me.

I've been trying to do
too much alone again.

Telling myself I can handle it.
That I don't need help from anyone.
That I should be able to figure it out by now.

But it's not working.

You never asked me
to be self-sufficient.

You asked me to stay near.

So here I am.

Not strong.
Not certain.

Just willing to lay it all
down at Your feet again.

Oh! Faithful God, help me trust
Your strength more than my own.

I need You.

March 13

Hi God, it's me.

Fear has been sitting
in the back of my mind again.

Telling me to shrink.
To play it safe. To stay quiet.

I know in my heart and in my soul
You didn't make me to live afraid.

You made me to live free.

Remind me of that, dear God,
when I start to believe the lies.

When I want to hold back.
When I want to disappear.

Remind me of the truth of You.

And of me too.

I am
created and made whole in Your light,
Your Love, Your everlasting power.

I am
to be seeing, to be heard, to be felt,
to transform and be transformed.

March 14

Hi God, it's me.

Thank You for
being my safe place.

The One I run to when
the world feels too loud.

When my own thoughts feel too heavy.
When my fears fill me with anxiety.

You never turn away from me.
Never ask me why I fear.

Oh! Faithful God!

You just open the door
and let me rest within You.

I need that today, God.

Not advice.
Not answers.

Just a place to exhale
and know I'm still loved.

Let me stay here a little longer,
in Your loving arms where I belong.

Oh! Faithful God, I need You.

March 15

Hi God, it's me.

I've been thinking
about purpose again.

Wondering
if I'm walking in it.

Worried I'm missing
something important.

What if I miss it?
What if I'm too late?
What if I'm off track?

I also think sometimes,
purpose isn't a finish line.

Maybe it's found in showing up in the small,
unnoticed moments. And in being faithful and true.

If that's true, I don't want to miss it.

Dear God, please help me
live with intention today.

Help me
to love well, to serve deeply,
to stay open to Your leading.

March 16

Hi God, it's me.

I haven't been feeling enough lately.

Like no matter how hard I try, I still fall
short and somehow become less than.

I know
that's not what You say nor think about me, dear God.
But the voices in my head don't always sound like You.

Dear God, can You please silence them?

The ones that tell me I have to earn worth.
The ones that keep me shrinking.

The ones that bond me
to fear, anxiety, and
helplessness.

Oh! Faithful God, remind me of who I am.
Who You say I am. Who You made me to be.

I am Yours.

Speak that truth over me
until it becomes the ground
I stand on, the peace I return to.

March 17

Hi God, it's me.

Thank You for the dreams
You've placed in my heart.

The ones that scare me.

The ones I've almost
talked myself out of.

Sometimes,
I wonder if I'm asking for too much.
But maybe I'm not asking boldly enough.

If they're from You, God,
I don't want to bury them.

I want to believe in them.

Nurture them.
Follow them.

See them come true.

I trust that what You've started in me,
You will finish in Your divine timing.

God, I believe in Your dreams for me.

I choose to walk toward them with courage,
trusting that every step I take is held by You.

March 18

Hi God, it's me.

I've been asking so many questions lately.

Question about who I am. About where I'm going.
About what truly matters in the quiet places of my life.

Honestly, I don't have many answers. And for the
first time, I'm starting to believe maybe that's okay.

Maybe my questions
are not signs of confusion.
But invitations into closeness.

Maybe they're the way You soften
my attention and draw me closer.

Somehow, even in the middle of uncertainty,
I feel You near; so near, so close to me, dear God.

Gentle. Patient. Present.

If clarity must come slowly, then give me peace as I wait.
God, give me grace to breathe between the unknowns.

I don't need to figure everything out. I only need to walk
with You. Dear God, I will wait for You as long as it takes.

Settle my spirit in Your timing.
Steady my heart in Your nearness.

Keep me close to You.

March 19

Hi God, it's me.

I'm noticing the more I quiet myself,
the more I can sense Your presence.

Not in sudden answers.

But in a soft awareness
settling over my spirit.

It feels
like You're teaching
me how to slow down.

How to trust the spaces between clarity. How to
breathe without rushing toward what I cannot yet see.

And in that stillness, I can feel something shifting:

a gentle renewal, a quiet beginning, a small
stirring of growth You're planting within me.

Help me stay present here:

in the middle, in the waiting,
in the slow miracle of being made new.

Dear God, let this season deepen my trust and
become a place of growth and quiet becoming.

I lean on You with a steadier, softer love.

March 20

Hi God, it's me.

I've been noticing how different life feels when I stop trying to force answers and simply let myself be led by You.

There's a calm I didn't expect to find. A softness settling into places that used to feel tense and restless.

Maybe this is what growth feels like.
Not loud or dramatic, but gentle, steady.

There's something sacred
unfolding beneath the surface.

I can sense You guiding me.

Not with pressure, but with presence.
Not with demands, but with peace.

Dear God, please help me keep leaning into that peace. Help me trust the quiet renewal happening inside of me, even on days when I can't see how everything fits together.

God, please teach me to move slowly, to move honestly, to move reverently, to move with You.

As I grow, let my life make room
for the person You're shaping me to be:

a little more open, a little more trusting; a lot like the one You envisioned since the beginning.

March 21

Hi God, it's me.

I woke up with a quiet awareness
that something in me is changing.

Not all at once.

Not in ways
I can easily explain.

But gently, steadily, like You're
softening the edges of my heart.

I don't know exactly
where this path is leading.

But I can feel You nudging me forward
with a peace that feels patient and kind.

Dear God, help me trust this slow becoming. Help me honor the small ways You're renewing me from within.

Even when I can't name the growth,
God, let me continue to walk with You.

Open.
Willing.
Trusting.

Quietly transformed by Your presence.

March 22

Hi God, it's me.

I've been thinking about how growth
often happens in the places no one sees.

In the thoughts I choose.
In the fears I release.

In the moments where I decide
to trust You instead of my doubts.

It's strange how something
so small can feel like a holy shift.

You're turning my heart toward a new
beginning without me even realizing it.

God, keep guiding me in these gentle ways.

Help me
notice the subtle renewal
You're planting in my spirit:

the hope returning, the peace settling, the strength
forming quietly beneath everything I don't yet understand.

Let today be
another step into the person
You're shaping me to become.

Softened, grounded, growing in Your light.

March 23

Hi God, it's me.

Lately I've been thinking
about the way relationships grow.

How they stretch me, mirror me, and reveal
parts of my heart I didn't know needed tending.

Sometimes it's beautiful.
Sometimes it's hard.

In all of it, I can sense You inviting me to love
with more honesty, more patience, more grace.

Dear God, teach me
how to grow in love
without losing myself.

Help me show up with softness and also with truth.
Help me listen well, speak kindly, and choose
connection especially when it's hard.

Growth requires courage.

Dear God,
grow me into someone
who loves boldly like You.

I want to love
courageously, steadily, gently;
from a place that's rooted in You.

March 24

Hi God, it's me.

Thank You for the people
You've placed in my life.

The ones who check in.
The ones who speak truth gently.
The ones who show me what love looks like.

I don't thank You for them enough.

But I see them.

I feel their presence.

I know they're a gift from You.

Please bless them, dear God.

Pour back into them what they so freely give.
Let them know they're seen and deeply loved.

March 25

Hi God, it's me.

Sometimes, I forget how far I've come.

I focus so much on what I still want to change,
that I look past the progress I've already made,
the progress You've already helped me make.

But today, I want to celebrate that.

The healing.
The growth.

The lessons learned.
The quiet bravery it took to stay.

Oh! Faithful God, thank You
for walking every step with me,
even the ones I had to crawl through.

Dear God, You never left.

You never let go.

I'm grateful for You.

My life unfolds in Your hands,
one healed place, one brave step,
one quiet miracle at a time.

March 26

Hi God, it's me.

I'm starting to see
little signs of growth.

Things that used to trigger me don't
shake me the same way anymore.

That's You, isn't it?

Softening my reactions.
Strengthening my spirit.

Healing me in ways
that only show up
as time goes by.

Thank You for the slow miracles. The ones
that don't shout but stay beside me quietly.

I'm learning how to hold joy again.

Dear God, I'm so in love with
what You're doing with me.

You're making me brand new.

I love this for me.

March 27

Hi God, it's me.

I tend to overlook
the small things.

The quiet joys.
The unnoticed mercies.

I saw them today and remembered how
much You care about the details of my life.

The way the sunlight landed on my face.
The unexpected moments of laughter.

The calm that came
after the moment I thought
I'd fall apart and never recover.

That was You.

It's always been You.

Oh! Faithful God, I thank You.

Keep opening my eyes
to the quiet ways You hold me,
so I never overlook the love that sustains me.

March 28

Hi God, it's me.

This month has taught me so much.

Some lessons arrived gently, wrapped in ease and softness.

Others came through aches and tears; stretching me, shaping me, asking me to trust You in places I didn't expect to grow.

You were in every lesson.

Every moment that asked me to become a little more honest, a little more open, a little more like the person You're forming.

And somehow, the hard things
made room for something better.

Something truer.
Something rooted in You.

Thank You for showing me growth doesn't
always look like success on the surface.

Sometimes it looks like staying.
Sometimes it looks like surrender.

Sometimes, it looks like healing
quietly where no one else can see.

Whatever it looks like, I want it with You.

Always with You.

March 29

Hi God, it's me.

Looking back on this month,
I see how far we've come.

Not just in what's happened.
But in who I'm becoming.

You've been
shaping me in ways
I couldn't see in the moment.

But I see them now.

Thank You
for staying close
while I grew in the dark.

I give You all my thanks
for not rushing the process.

For being a patient Father
to a restless human heart.

Dear God, You are
faithful and true.

Keep me close.
Keep me growing.
Keep me Yours.

March 30

Hi God, it's me.

Before this month ends,
I want to lay it all at Your feet.

The wins.
The worries.

The days I loved and
the ones I barely survived.

All of them are Yours.

I trust that You'll use them
for my good and for Your glory.
For something I can't imagine yet.

God, thank You for walking with me.

Every step. Every breath.
Every light. Every love.

You are everything to me.

I rest my whole heart
in the safety of
Your love.

March 31

Hi God, it's me.

A new month is almost here.

But before I turn the page,
I just want to say one thing:

Thank You.

For not giving up on me.
For carrying me through.
For loving me in the in-between.

Whatever tomorrow holds, I know I won't
face it alone because You're already there.

Dear God, wherever You
go is where I want to be.

Lead me into the days ahead
with Your peace as my anchor.

Your voice is my guide.

Your presence is the holy place
where my heart finally rests.

I'm stepping forward with You.

God,
I'm trusting, open, and ready for
whatever Your love will make new.

APRIL

Presence & Stillness

There's a quiet invitation woven through this month.

A gentle urging to slow your steps and listen for God in the spaces between your breaths. Presence is not found in noise or movement. It rises in stillness, where your spirit can finally hear the whisper beneath the world's demands and sense the tender way God has been guiding you all along.

This is where God meets you.

Not in striving, but in surrender.

You don't have to travel far to find God. He's in the hush of the morning, in the softness of your sigh, in the moments when you stop trying to hold everything together. And each time your heart loosens, your body remembers how to rest.

Stillness is not emptiness. It's awareness.

It's how you open the door for God to draw nearer.

Stillness is the sacred ground where you remember God has always been close. Let this month remind you that peace is never earned through effort. It's received through presence. The world may pull at your attention, but your soul knows the way home. And in the quiet, you rediscover the strength that comes only from sitting gently in God's light.

You were not created to live in hurry.

You were created to live holy.

So breathe deeper. Move slower. Notice the divine woven into the ordinary. The light resting on your face. The quiet forming between your thoughts. The gift of simply being alive. God is here, closer than your next heartbeat, closer than your next breath. God is your sanctuary, your stillness, your peace.

This is the month you choose presence over pressure.

Holiness begins the moment you simply sit and be still with God.

April 1

Hi God, it's me.

I want to begin this
month with stillness.

No urgency.
No noise.

Just awareness of You.

I've been moving so fast,
chasing goals and answers,
that I forgot what it feels like
to simply be in Your presence.

Dear God, please slow me
down from the inside out.

Still my mind.
Quiet my fears.

Bring my scattered
spirit back to center.

This month, I don't want to miss You
because I was too busy looking ahead.

Please be with me, God.

Here and now.

April 2

Hi God, it's me.

The world is so loud.

Sometimes I forget I have the choice
to step back and enter into Your divine peace.

I don't
want to be driven
by constant urgency.

I want to be drawn by Your Spirit.

Gently.
Faithfully.
Day by day.

Teach me how to choose stillness even when
everything around me feels like it's spinning.

Let me find You.

Not in the chaos.
But in the calm.

Dear God, You are my quiet place.

My safe home in a noisy world.

April 3

Hi God, it's me.

I want to be more aware
of the way the sun
feels on my skin.

Of
the way peace moves
through a quiet room.

And of the way You whisper in my heart
when I'm finally still enough to hear.

I don't want to miss the
little ways You show up.

You're always speaking.

Always near.

God, please slow me down today
so I don't rush past the miracles.

In all things, I want to see You.

April 4

Hi God, it's me.

It's hard for me to rest sometimes.
Not just physically, but in my spirit.

In the deep places where I hold
tension and keep proving I'm okay.

I don't want
to perform for peace.

I want to receive it.

You have more than enough for me.
So I'm breathing slower today and resting.

Not because I have everything figured out.
But because I don't and You're still here.

Heavenly Father God,
thank You for making a bed
in the palm of Your hands for me.

Thank You for a home in You where
I can lay down and rest without worry.

Dear God, I rest in You.

April 5

Hi God, it's me.

I woke up feeling unsettled.

Like I forgot something important; like
I'm behind on a race I never meant to run.

Maybe the thing I forgot
was to simply sit with You.

To pause.
To breathe.

To remember I am not my pace.

Dear God, please remind me today
that presence is not wasted time.

Please remind me of the truth.

Stillness is not laziness.

My soul needs quiet time
as much as my body needs rest.

Be my reset, Father God.

Settle me into the pace that
comes from Your peace alone.

April 6

Hi God, it's me.

I carry more
than people know.

A quiet weight.

A hidden pressure to keep going
even when I'm tired on the inside.

You see it.

And that alone brings me comfort.

You
don't ask me
to push through.

You ask me to come close.

So here I am again, asking for peace.

Not the kind I have to earn.
But the kind You give freely.

Meet me here, Restful God.

In this still moment that I've
carved out just to be with You.

Settle my soul in Your calm.

April 7

Hi God, it's me.

There's something sacred
about the way You move slowly.

The way You never rush healing.
The way You never force growth.

You just stay.
You just love.

I want to carry
that with me today.

To listen longer.
To move with intention.
To respond with gentleness.

Let me reflect the pace of heaven
in the middle of this very human day.
Let my life be a soft echo of Your presence.

Stay close to me, God.

Wrap me in the nearness that steadies
my spirit and quiets every anxious place.

Let Your presence be the rhythm that guides
my steps, the peace that anchors my breath.

God, You're the holiness woven
through every moment I live.

April 8

Hi God, it's me.

I've been thinking about
what it means to be here.

Not just
physically present,
but emotionally.

Spiritually.

Available for connection.

I don't want
to go through life half-awake,
half-trusting, half-listening to You.

Wake me up gently, God.

To the moment I'm in.
To the breath I'm breathing.
To the sacredness of this exact day.

I don't want to miss it
while I chase something else.

This moment matters
because You're in it.

Dear God, I am here,
fully present with You.

April 9

Hi God, it's me.

I've been holding
my breath lately.

Waiting for the next thing.
Anticipating what could go wrong.

And I'm tired.

I'm tired of being tense. Of expecting the worst.
Of always feeling like peace is always out of reach for me.

I want to breathe again.

To inhale grace.
To exhale fear.

You are my safety, God.

Not circumstances.
Not control.

Just You.

I breathe in Your presence today. The kind that
reminds me I am held, I am loved, I am safe in You.

Every inhale draws me deeper into Your peace; and
every exhale release what was never mine to carry.

God, be the holy air around me, within me, and for me.

April 10

Hi God, it's me.

Sometimes I struggle to feel like I belong in rooms, in conversations, in the rhythms of my own life.

But in Your presence, I fit without trying.

I rest without earning.
I'm held without fear.

With You, belonging isn't a place I search for.

It's a presence I enter, holy
nearness that knows me.

It's a love
that welcomes me
before I say a word.

Sweet, Loving God, draw me
deeper into that truth today.

Your presence is the space where my heart
feels safe, seen, and completely accepted.

Dear God, I belong with You.

Fully.
Completely.

Always.

April 11

Hi God, it's me.

I've been distracted lately.

Reaching for things
that can't satisfy me.

Trying to fill spaces that
only You were made for.

Dear God, please bring me back.

Back to stillness.
Back to the truth.

Back to the gentle rhythm
of walking and living with You.

Help me put down everything
I picked up that's weighing me down.

I want to be light again.
I want to be close again.
I want to be with You.

I want You.

Only You.

April 12

Hi God, it's me.

Some days I feel
like I'm in between.

Not where I used to be,
not quite where I want to be.

It's easy to rush past this part and look for the next
thing instead of staying present in the becoming.

But this quiet middle
is where You meet me:

in the pause, in the uncertainty, in the
tender space where transformation begins.

You do
beautiful things
in the in-between.

Help me see that, Lord.

Teach me to rest here,
to breathe here, to trust that Your hands
are shaping me in ways I cannot yet see.

Dear God, help me embrace
this middle space as holy ground.

April 13

Hi God, it's me.

Sometimes, it's hard
for me to accept silence.

I want answers.
I want clear signs.

I want things
I can hold on to.

In my heart
I know without a doubt You
don't always speak in volume.

Sometimes,
You just sit beside me.

Unmoving.
Unshaken.

Let that be enough today.

I find comfort not in what You say,
but in the fact that You're with me.

Your nearness is all I need.

April 14

Hi God, it's me.

I woke up anxious
for no particular reason.

Just
a heaviness
I can't explain.

Dear God, I know
You know what it is.

You know how to unravel it.
How to hold it without judgment.

Please wrap me in Your peace today.
The kind that doesn't need a reason.

The kind of peace that covers
me before the day even begins.

God, You are my calm.
You're the peace I crave.

April 15

Hi God, it's me.

We're
halfway through the month
and I feel something shifting.

Not outside of me, but inside.

Like maybe
peace is no longer
something I reach for.

Maybe it's something that's
taking root deep inside my heart.

Thank You for quiet growth.

I give thanks for the kind of change
that doesn't need to be seen
to be holy and sacred.

I'm learning to live
in rhythm with You.

God, I'm immensely grateful
for transforming through You.

April 16

Hi God, it's me.

There's a difference
between silence
and stillness.

Silence can sometimes be empty.

But stillness is always full.

Stillness
is full of awareness,
of presence, of You.

Let me choose stillness today.
Not to escape, but to tune in.

God, open my eyes to see and to give thanks
for what You're doing beneath the surface.

I don't want to miss You.

Not in this season.
Not in this breath.

With You, I am.

With You, I will always be.

April 17

Hi God, it's me.

There's so much
I don't understand.

About timing.
About waiting.

About why some prayers
take much longer than others.

I'm learning
peace isn't always
found in the answers.

It's found in You.

So even if nothing changes
today, let me still feel held.

Still feel loved.
Still feel found.

You're all I need.

April 18

Hi God, it's me.

Some days feel heavy
for no clear reason.

Like my spirit
is dragging behind
my body.

I know You don't need me
to have a reason to come to You.

So here I am.

Just needing comfort.
Just needing closeness.

Dear God,
please meet me
in this moment.

No fixing.
No pressure.

Just love.

April 19

Hi God, it's me.

I keep thinking peace means
everything around me is calm.

But You keep showing
me peace starts inside.

With trust.
With surrender.
With presence.

So today, I'm letting go of what I can't
control and holding on to You instead.

That's the kind of peace I want.

The kind
that doesn't depend on perfect
conditions but on Your perfect love.

Your peace is with me.

Settling my spirit, steadying my breath,
guiding my heart back to You again and again.

Always.

April 20

Hi God, it's me.

Sometimes, I forget
You're in the ordinary.

In the dishes I'm washing.
In the silence between texts.
In the rhythm of my footsteps.

I keep searching for You
in mountaintop moments
when You're already here,
so quiet, so close, so warm.

I want to live today
knowing You're beside me.

Not
just during prayer,
but in everything.

God, help me recognize the sacred in the routine.
Help me pay attention to the soft ways You speak.

I don't need a miracle to know You're near.
I just need to slow down enough to notice.

God, let me find You
in the details I overlook.

You're beauty in the background.
You're with me in every breath.

April 21

Hi God, it's me.

You hold time for me.
You're never in a rush.

You never roll Your eyes when
I bring the same fears again.

You just stay.

Present. Patient. Loving.

That kind of love quiets my soul.

It slows my racing thoughts.
It gives me room to exhale.

I don't want to bring You perfect prayers.
I want to bring You the raw and honest ones.

The kind that sounds like breathing.

The kind that says, "I'm here," even when
I don't have anything profound to offer You.

You meet me in that.
God, You always do.

Simple and sincere.

Dear God, that's the kind of
intimacy I treasure with You.

April 22

Hi God, it's me.

I want to be more mindful.

Not just aware
of my surroundings,
but aware of You.

Your Spirit is nudging me to pause, to breathe,
to respond with softness instead of reaction.

I rush through so much, and often miss the
moments that could change everything.

God, slow me down from the inside.
Not just in my body. But in my spirit.

Let me walk into every conversation, into every task,
into every room, as someone who's been with You.

Let me carry peace that doesn't proclaim itself.
The peace that doesn't need to prove itself.

I want to reflect the divine peace of You.

Peace that just lives,
just breathes, just loves.

Peace that just is.

You.

April 23

Hi God, it's me.

You've been teaching
me how to live slow.

How to let go of urgency and
stop apologizing for needing space.

I'm starting to love it.

This space where I can breathe;
this awareness that allows me
to feel everything more fully.

I notice the flowers.

The way light rests on walls.
The softness in a friend's eyes.

I notice You.

You've been here all along.

Now that I've slowed
down, I see You again.

Let me live this way, always.
Tuned in. Unhurried. Present.

This is what my soul was made for.

Stillness is my home with You.

April 24

Hi God, it's me.

Sometimes, I mistake stillness for passivity.
Like if I'm not striving, I'm falling behind.

In my heart, I know for sure
stillness with You is not inactivity.

It's deep work.

It's healing I can't always see.

Help me trust
what You're doing
beneath the surface.

When things look quiet,
remind me that seeds grow in silence.
Transformation happens without applause.

I rest in the unseen without
rushing to prove I'm growing.

You're doing something in me.

I don't
need to rush it
to believe it's real.

I trust You.

April 25

Hi God, it's me.

I want to remain with You.

Not check in and
then drift off again.

Not call You when I need help
and forget You when I'm fine.

Teach me what it means to abide.

To stay.

To live with an open door
between my heart and Yours.

Help me return to You
all throughout the day.

In the car,
in the grocery line,
in the silence before sleep.

You're not just a moment.

You are my home.

Keep me rooted in You, God.

April 26

Hi God, it's me.

I thought peace was something
I had to go find somewhere far.

But now I know, You already gave it to me.
I've just been too distracted to receive it.

Too focused
on what I don't have
to notice what's already here.

So today, I'm opening my hands.

I'm letting go of the need to fix things.
To be everywhere. To know everything.

Your peace fills the empty space.

It takes up room in my mind,
in my schedule and in my heart.

Dear God, You give me peace.
Your presence is the calm I carry.

April 27

Hi God, it's me.

I want to stay soft
when the world feels sharp.

It hardens me
if I'm not careful.

That's why I keep
running back to You.

Not to be toughened.
But to be tender again.

Dear God,
You've taught me
tenderness isn't weakness.

It's the strength to stay open
in a world that tells me to shut down.

Let me be someone who doesn't numb their
feelings, but learns how to hold them with You.

You shape my heart
with a gentleness that steadies me,
a holiness that softens me from within.

Lord, my Master, my King, my God,
my softness is holy in Your presence;
my love is bold in its gentleness with You.

April 28

Hi God, it's me.

I can feel myself
slipping back into business.

Into productivity over presence.
Into autopilot like a lifeless machine.

I don't want to lose what You've
been teaching me this month.

Please bring me
back to stillness.

Let it anchor me.

Let it slow my reactions
and deepen my awareness.

You don't measure me
by what I accomplish.

You draw near.
You love me.

That's enough.

I end this month in the quiet
You've cultivated in me.

Held. Unhurried.
At home in Your peace.

April 29

Hi God, it's me.

This month has
been a quiet gift.

Not loud.
Not flashy.

But grounding.

Gentle.
Transformational.

You've met me
in morning silence
and evening stillness.

You've reminded me peace
is not something I chase.

It's a gift I must always
choose and treasure.

Thank You
for shifting me in ways
I didn't even know I needed.

This is more than a moment.
This is a new way of being.

Every month, I'll keep choosing You.

April 30

Hi God, it's me.

Before I close this month,
I just want to say thank You.

For the quiet.
For the pause.
For the breath.

For the slowness
that settled my soul.

You didn't need noise to speak.
You didn't need a storm to teach me.

You
met me in the breath
between distractions.

You changed everything in me.

I don't want to return to rushing.
I want to live in rhythm with You.

Let May be rooted in
everything April gave me.

Let me remain present.
Let me remain Yours.

MAY

Purpose & Identity

You were created on purpose, for purpose.

Before you ever took a breath, Heaven whispered your name with intention, weaving eternity into the fabric of your being. Before the world named you by what you do, God named you by who you are: beloved, chosen, seen.

This month is a homecoming to that truth, a gentle return to the center of your being, where your worth is not measured by accomplishment but by belonging. God is drawing you back to the identity that has always been yours in Him.

Purpose is not always loud.

Sometimes it whispers through ordinary days, through quiet acts of love, through faithfulness in places no one sees. It's less about arriving somewhere and more about being aligned through your heart, spirit, and soul with the One who made you.

Let your purpose rise softly within you like morning light, revealing what has been sacred all along. You don't have to search for your identity; you only have to remember it. Beneath the noise, beneath the comparison, there's a steady voice reminding you, *You are Mine.*

Let God's truth settle in your spirit like a holy stillness, anchoring you in the love that cannot be taken.

When you live from that truth, the smallest moments carry divinity. Every breath becomes a quiet prayer, every step a reminder that God walks with you in the unseen. Let this month be your invitation to walk in confidence. Not in your strength, but in your divine design. Stand in the light of who God says you are and let every step you take become an echo of His love through you.

May your journey through May be a sacred unfolding, a gentle unveiling of the glory God placed within you. This is the sacred work of May: to remember who you are in God. And as you remember, may Heaven remind you again and again that your life is a living testimony of His perfect divine will.

May 1

Hi God, it's me.

I want to start this
month with clarity.

Not about every step.
But about who I am.

There are
so many voices
trying to define me.

Success. Status.
Image. Pressure.

But I want Your voice
to be the one that sticks.

Who do You say I am?

I want to build from that.

Live from that.

Wake up and breathe that in
before taking in anything else.

Let this be the month I stop second-guessing
who I am and start standing in who You created.

I am Yours.

May 2

Hi God, it's me.

I've spent so much time
trying to be what others need,
trying to be what the world expects,
what I thought I had to be to be loved.

I miss myself.

The one You made
before the fear crept in.

Before comparison
clouded everything.

Dear God, can You please
bring me back to the real me?

The authentic me?

The one who's already enough.
The one who doesn't need fixing.

Dear God, please help me strip away
the pressure and return to the core.

That's where You are.

And where You are
is where I want to be.

I need You.

May 3

Hi God, it's me.

Sometimes,
I feel behind.

Like I missed something.
Like I'm late to my own purpose.

I know that's not
how You see me.

You're never rushed.

You're never
disappointed
with my pace.

God, please remind me today that
purpose isn't just in big moments.

It's in how I speak to others.

How I love.

How I show up even
when no one's watching.

I don't want to chase tasks and
miss the calling right in front of me.

Faithful and Holy God, please
help me align my will with Yours.

May 4

Hi God, it's me.

I've been
questioning
everything lately.

My path. My goals.

Even my voice.

I've also been wondering that maybe
those questions aren't signs of failure.

Maybe they're just signs
that I care deeply about
living on purpose.

Dear God, can You please help me
discern what's from You and what's not?

Help me let go of everything that's distracting me
from becoming who you made me to be, who I truly am.

I want to be aligned, dear God.

Not just busy.

Not just "doing enough."

Aligned.

With You. With truth. With myself.

May 5

Hi God, it's me.

Today I want to
believe I'm called.

Not just talented.
Not just helpful.

But chosen.

Set apart.
Held in Your vision.

I want to walk through today
as someone who carries purpose.

In small and big spaces, let me not
underestimate how You can use me.

In a text.
In a meeting.

In a whisper of encouragement
that changes someone's day.

Purpose isn't always loud.

But it's always powerful
when it comes from You.

I want to live in purpose with You.

May 6

Hi God, it's me.

I've
been waiting
for a big sign.

Something clear.
Something loud.

All the while, You're
waiting for me just to start.

To trust that You'll guide me as I go.

I don't want the fear of doing it wrong
to stop me from doing anything at all.

Give me courage, dear God.

To begin.
To believe.

To take one faithful step when
I don't know what comes next.

Help me to trust and believe
You're with me on the path
leading every step I take.

May 7

Hi God, it's me.

I want to love who You made me to be.

Not just tolerate myself.
Not just manage my flaws.

But really love the way You handcrafted me.

Sometimes, it's hard.

The world tells me to
change before I'm lovable.

But You say I'm loved *now*.

Let this truth settle
deep into my identity.

Into how I walk into rooms. Into how
I talk to myself when no one else is around.

I am lovingly and wonderfully made
by the God of love, the God of light.

The One who fills the world with awe.

My Creator is the King of Kings.

Master of the Universe.

I am His beloved child.

May 8

Hi God, it's me.

I've been trying
so hard to "get it right."

To make the best decision. To avoid mistakes.
To live a life that's impressive and meaningful.

I'm learning that purpose
isn't found in perfection.

It's found in surrender.

You're not asking me to have it all figured out.

You're
asking me to walk with You,
to trust You with the process,
to be obedient even when I'm unsure.

Today,
I release the pressure
to have a perfect plan.

I just want to be faithful to Your voice.

I'll take small steps.

Quiet ones.
Honest ones.

And if all I do today is stay close to You, let that be enough.

May 9

Hi God, it's me.

Sometimes I feel invisible.
Like what I do doesn't matter.

Sometimes it's as if
no one sees the effort
or the heart behind it.

But You see me.

You see everything.

Every quiet *yes*.

Every private surrender.

Every moment I choose to show up anyway.

God, remind me today that significance
doesn't come from being seen by everyone.

It comes from being known by You.

Let me be more committed to Your
calling than to any kind of validation.

You see me.

In Your gaze, I remember who I am.

May 10

Hi God, it's me.

Comparison crept in again.

I didn't even notice at first.

I started measuring
my worth against
someone else.

I don't want to live that way.

I don't want to miss my lane
while looking over my shoulder.

You created me with intention.

On purpose.
For purpose.

Help me refocus today.

God, please remind me what You've given me.

My voice.
My timing.
My calling.

That's more than enough.

Let me stay in my lane, rooted in Your grace
and at peace with how You've written my story.

May 11

Hi God, it's me.

I'm realizing how many stories
I've believed that weren't from You.

Stories that said I'm not enough.

That I'm disqualified.
That I'm too much.
That I missed it.

These were never
the stories of You for me.

I want to live
from the stories
You've written for me.

So today, I lay down the lies.

The ones I picked up as a child.
The ones I rehearsed as an adult.
The ones that tried to shrink me.

Speak truth louder, dear God.

Speak it to my heart.
Shout it to my soul.

Let Your words shape my worth.

Let me become the story You've been telling all along.

May 12

Hi God, it's me.

There's something inside
me that longs to create.

To express.

To bring beauty into the world.

Sometimes, I question
if it's worth doing
if it's not seen by many.

But You, dear God!

You remind me that I'm not here to create for applause.
I create because I'm made in the image of the Creator.

Holy, Creative God,
let my work be worship.
Let it reflect Your goodness.

Let it heal what needs healing and bring joy where it's needed.
Whatever I create, dear God, let it return to You as worship.

Let Heaven recognize it as Yours.

May 13

Hi God, it's me.

I want to show up fully today.

Not as a version of myself
that I think people want.

But
as the person
You've made.

It's tempting to shrink.

To tone it down.
To blend in.

And so, I must remind myself of the truth.

You didn't make me for invisibility.
You made me to carry light.

Powerful God,
please help me walk boldly
without needing to perform.

Let my confidence
come not from perfection,
but from being rooted in You.

I am who You say I am.

May 14

Hi God, it's me.

I've been
thinking about legacy.

What I'll leave behind.
What really matters.

I don't want to just build a life.

I want to build a life that reflects You.

One
where love is felt,
where truth is known,
where healing is offered.

God, teach me to live intentionally.
To make every moment count without
exhausting myself with the need to prove.

Let my purpose be found
not in doing more,
but in loving well.

Let that be the legacy I leave.

Love that looks like You.

The kind that reminds the world of You.

May 15

Hi God, it's me.

Sometimes I wonder
if I'm making a difference.

I question if what I'm doing matters.
If my life is leaving any kind of mark.

But You constantly remind me
that purpose isn't always loud.

It's not always
a platform or spotlight.

Sometimes, it's faithfulness.

Sometimes, it's showing up
on the days I'd rather stay in bed.

Sometimes, it's listening. Being kind.
Choosing love when it's inconvenient.

That's the kind of purpose I want.

The kind that pleases You,
even if no one else sees it.

God, I trust You're using me;
writing Your goodness quietly
between the lines of my life.

May 16

Hi God, it's me.

I've been carrying
these question
in my chest:

What if I mess it up?
What if I'm not enough?

What if I disappoint You?
What if I try and still fall short?

I know You don't base Your love
on outcomes or performances.

God, You've called me before
I ever accomplished anything.

So remind me again today.

My worth isn't fragile.
My identity isn't earned.

I am Yours.

And that's not changing.

Faithful God, let that truth fill me
until doubt no longer feels like home,
and peace becomes the air I breathe.

May 17

Hi God, it's me.

I feel a pull toward something more
but I'm not sure what that means yet.

It's like my heart knows but
my mind hasn't caught up yet.

And part of me is scared.

To step out.
To stretch.
To trust.

I don't want to ignore Your voice
just because the path feels unclear.

So, speak to me in a way I recognize.

Lead me gently.

Give me courage to say *yes*
even while I'm still trembling.

I believe You're preparing me for something I can't see yet.
I want to be ready for whatever You have in store for me.

God, please keep my heart soft,
and my spirit willing to follow.

My whole being leans into the way You lead.

May 18

Hi God, it's me.

Help me unlearn what isn't true.

All the ways I've measured success.
All the rules I made up to feel safe.
All the habits that kept me hidden.

I want to build a life that reflects
freedom, authenticity, and happiness.

A life that actually feels like mine.

Not the version
I think people expect.

Strip it all back, dear God.

Until all that's left is truth.

And You.
And me.

Free and fully known.

United in love.

The version of me You've loved all along.

May 19

Hi God, it's me.

Comparison is sneaky.

It wraps itself
around my confidence
when I'm not paying attention.

You didn't make me
to be someone else.

You made me to be unique.
You made me to create something
no one else can do exactly like me.

Therefore, I'm choosing to
believe today, I am enough.

That my pace is okay.
That my story matters.
That me and You is all I need.

Help me celebrate others
without questioning myself.

You didn't make me to compete.
You made me to contribute.

And that's who I want to be.

Rooted in You. Whole in my own lane.
Content in the miracle of simply being Yours.

May 20

Hi God, it's me.

Sometimes I wait for permission.

To speak up.
To move forward.
To believe in myself.

Maybe You've already given me that. Maybe I don't need to keep asking when You've already said *yes*.

Yes to growth.
Yes to purpose.
Yes to creating.

Yes to using the gifts You gave me.

So today, I say *yes* too.

To courage. To clarity. To love.
To the calling I keep trying to shrink from.

Shine Your light on me, dear God.

Lead me where Your presence already is.
Reveal me to the places where You abide.

My steps echo Your will.
My words carry Your heart.

My life is the *yes* that brings You glory.

May 21

Hi God, it's me.

You've been reminding me
I don't have to be everything.

I don't have to do it all.

I'm not more valuable
when I'm exhausted.

Thank You for teaching me
purpose doesn't require burnout.

My divine calling includes rest.

God, please help me to steward my energy.
To honor my limits, to let grace set the pace.

Faithful God, please let my identity rest
not in what I produce but in who I am:

loved, enough, held by You eternally.

Holiness
isn't in how much I give,
but in how deeply I abide.

Let me find You in quiet moments and gentle pauses.
And when I forget, dear God, please call me back.

To peace. To presence. To You.

May 22

Hi God, it's me.

I've been wondering:

what if I'm already
walking in my purpose,
but too distracted to see it?

Too focused on what's next.
Too caught up in what's missing.
Too consumed by what others are doing.

God, please help me slow down and notice.
I want to see what You've put in front of me.

The small ways I get to serve.
The sacredness of my ordinary life.

Purpose isn't a destination.

It's the way I show up here and now.

Help me show up well, dear God.
In every day. In every way.

Be near me, God.

In the pauses between purpose and
proof. In the moments I feel unseen.

Remind me You walk beside me,
turning my steps into sacred ground.

May 23

Hi God, it's me.

There's a fire burning bright inside me.
A longing to do something meaningful.

My heart
desires to build something lasting,
to be part of something that matters.

I don't want to chase greatness for my own
glory. I want to live for something deeper.

Wider.
Eternal.
Powerful.

Dear God, please show me how to use what
You've given me without losing sight of You.

Let my ambition be anchored in
grace; my goals be guided by love.

Whatever I build, let it reflect You.

And when my hands grow tired,
remind me You are the builder.

I'm simply the vessel, creating from
the breath You placed within me.

My heart is humble. My spirit is surrendered.
My work is a quiet offering of love back to You.

May 24

Hi God, it's me.

I'm starting to believe
I don't have to be anyone else.

I'm starting to believe I can show up as myself:
honest, unsure, growing and still be used by You.

God, thank You for never asking me to become
someone different before You called me worthy.

You see
who I am and who
I'm becoming all at once.

Dear God, please teach me
how to show up with boldness.

To be fully me, in love, in light, in power.
Teach me how to be who You created me to be.

When doubt tries to whisper,
remind me I'm already Yours.

I was chosen long before time begun.

Wrap me in Your peace when I forget my own light.
Let my becoming be holy, and my being be enough.

Dear God,
keep me close to You;
steady, seen, sacred.

May 25

Hi God, it's me.

I've been thinking about
what it means to live a full life.

Not a perfect one.
Not a busy one.

Just a life full of love, truth, and purpose.

Help me define "success" by Your standards.

Not by what I can achieve.
But by how well I love.

I wish
to be known not just for what I do.
But for who I am and who I reflect.

Shape my life around what matters most.

Let me live full, not frantic.

When the world pulls me toward more
and faster, remind me to return to You.

To the quiet center of my soul:

where love is enough, where grace is abundant, and where fullness is found not in what I hold, but in who holds me.

You.

May 26

Hi God, it's me.

It's hard to let go of the
version of life I imagined.

The one where everything made sense.
The one where timelines lined up, where
everything happened when I wanted it to.

But then again, maybe that version was too
small. Maybe You're writing a better story.

Sweet, Loving God, help me trust that
letting go doesn't mean giving up.

It means making room.

Room for grace.
Room for growth.

Room for something greater.

I want to live open-handed with You.

When my hands tremble, hold them steady. When my heart
aches for what was, please remind me of what's being born.

Teach me to rest in the unfolding of Your will.
To trust that even in the unknown, I am safely led.

Every letting go is an act of worship.
Every empty space fills up with You.

May 27

Hi God, it's me.

Thank You for the gifts
You placed in me.

The ones I didn't think were valuable.
The ones I'm still discovering.
The ones I used to hide.

You saw purpose in me
before I ever saw it in myself.

God, please help me use what I've been given.

Not out of pressure.
But out of love.

Not to be impressive.
But to be impactful.

You are the source of everything great in me.
I want to give greatness back to the world.

So breathe through me, God.

Let every word, every offering,
become a reflection of Your heart.

Let my life sing what my lips cannot say:
that all I am and all I give belong to You.

May 28

Hi God, it's me.

Some days I feel clear.
Other days I feel lost.

Yet when I question my path,
I never question Your presence.

I thank You from my heart and soul for being with me in the unknown. In the figuring it out. In the becoming.

Purpose doesn't mean every day feels certain.
It just means I'm choosing to trust You as I go.

Dear God, lead me one step at a time.

I don't need the whole map.
Just Your hand in mine.

When I can't see the way, let me feel You near.
Whisper peace into my pace, stillness into my soul.

God, remind me
faith isn't about seeing clearly,
but about resting safely in You.

May 29

Hi God, it's me.

I've learned a lot this month.

About who I am.
About what matters.
About how I want to live.

I don't want to forget it.

Let these lessons sink deep. Let them
become the foundation I keep building on.

You've reminded me that I don't have
to search far to find my purpose.

It's already here.

In how I love.
In whom I serve.

In the way I walk with You.

As I step into what's next, help me
carry these truths with reverence.

Let them shape my heart before they shape my plans.
Keep me rooted in Your wisdom, and open to Your whispers.

Dear God, every lesson written this month
was You, writing sacred verses on my soul.

May 30

Hi God, it's me.

Before this month ends,
I want to honor who I'm becoming.

I may not be where I want to be.
But I'm not where I used to be either.

You've been faithful in the process.

Patient in the growing pains.

Present in every moment of doubt and hope.

Thank You for revealing more of my identity.
Thank You for walking me into purpose
with tenderness, truth, and love.

I'm still becoming
and You're still here.

As I step forward, dear God,
keep shaping me in Your image.

Let every breath become worship;
every becoming, a homecoming to You.

Settle my soul in the truth
that I'm never unfinished.

Only unfolding in Your hands.

May 31

Hi God, it's me.

I close this month
with a quiet heart.

Grateful.
Centered.

Rooted in who I am
because of who You are.

I don't need all the answers.
I don't need every door open.

I just need
to stay aligned
with You.

That's where my identity is safe.
That's where I feel most at home.
That's where my purpose makes sense.

Let me carry that into whatever comes next.

As a new month begins, keep me anchored in Your presence. Stillness is my strength and trust is my song.

Whatever awaits beyond this page, meet me there, God.

In love, in light, in the gentle rhythm of Your will.

JUNE

Joy & Celebration

Joy is the quiet song the soul sings when it remembers the nearness of God. It rises gently and without effort, blooming in the very places where sorrow once tried to take root. Joy doesn't wait for perfect timing. It appears like light slipping through a window, surprising you with warmth you didn't expect. It's God reminding you, softly and faithfully, that goodness finds you everywhere.

This month is an opening; an invitation to breathe lighter, to notice beauty before it passes, to let laughter return to places inside you that have been silent for way too long. You're being asked to soften, to allow your spirit to be lifted by the simple graces that surround you.

Sometimes God meets you in grandeur, but often He reveals Himself in the smallest moments, the kinds that whisper instead of shout.

Joy is not the absence of sorrow. It's the courage to keep your eyes open for God's hand even in the midst of it. It's the soft resilience that reminds you love still lives inside you, untouched and unforgotten. When you lift your gaze toward Heaven, remember that God's joy is planted within you like an anchor, steady and unmoving. It's not fleeting. It's foundational, a truth that holds you when everything else feels uncertain.

Celebration is not reserved for the grand or the extraordinary. It's found in the tenderness of everyday life. God delights when you delight. Heaven leans close when you rediscover wonder in the sunlight or gratitude in an ordinary morning. Every smile becomes a prayer. Every peaceful breath, a quiet offering of thanksgiving rising back to God. Celebration is simply recognizing that God is here, and that His presence is reason enough to rejoice.

This is the rhythm of June: to rejoice, to remember, to live as one who is deeply loved. Let joy catch you off guard. Let celebration become your quiet worship, a way of saying "thank You" simply by being present to the life you're living. You don't have to earn any of this; you only have to notice it, receive it, and let it open your heart a little more each day.

June 1

Hi God, it's me.

A new month is here.

I can feel You inviting
me to smile again.

To breathe deep into my belly
and loosen my grip on what's heavy.

Joy is sunlight touching the
parts of me that forgot warmth.

And I'm so glad because I know
joy isn't something I have to chase.

It's something I choose.

Something You placed within me.

So today, I open my heart to it.

To laughter. To gratitude. To the quiet
ways You remind me life is still beautiful.

Thank You for every reason to rejoice,
even the ones hidden in ordinary days.

I'm ready to celebrate again, dear God,
not because everything is perfect,
but because You are.

June 2

Hi God, it's me.

I woke up today
with a softness
in my heart.

A
reminder that peace
is also a kind of joy.

Not loud.
Not showy.

Just steady.

The kind that hums beneath
everything when life feels uncertain.

Thank You for mornings that feel like mercy.
Thank You for air that tastes like beginning again.
For the quiet gift of being here alive, breathing, loved.

God, help me carry this peace
through every moment today.

May it settle in my spirit
like sunlight on still water,
proof that You are near.

June 3

Hi God, it's me.

I went outside today and felt
joy blooming in the simplest things.

The trees swayed as
they were praising You.

The breeze
brushed against my skin,
a quiet reminder I'm alive.

Sunlight
stretched across the ground
like laughter made visible.

You made all of this.

Not just to exist.
But to bring delight.

God, thank You for beauty that
doesn't wait for a reason to appear.

Thank You for teaching me joy is a way
of seeing, a way of remembering You are here.

My eyes stay open to every glimpse of Your goodness.
When I notice You, my heart can't help but celebrate.

Joy. Joy. Joy.

June 4

Hi God, it's me.

I laughed today.
Really laughed.

And for a moment,
I forgot to be careful.
I forgot to hold back.

It felt like freedom.
It felt like You.

Thank You, God, for the kind of joy
that bubbles up without permission.

For moments that lift the weight
I didn't realize I was still carrying.

Dear God, please remind me that laughter is holy too, a sacred melody of gratitude that rises straight to Heaven.

Let my life sound like that every day.

Unforced.
Unashamed.

Alive with joy.

June 5

Hi God, it's me.

Joy found me today
in the most ordinary moment.

Not in a grand surprise,
but in the calm of my own breath,
in sunlight rested gently on my hands.

It felt small, but it filled the room.

God, thank You for reminding
me joy doesn't always shout.

Sometimes,
it simply whispers,
I am here.

Help me to honor
those whispers, God.

To hold onto peace
as something sacred.

Because even in the quiet,
there's always a reason
to celebrate You.

June 6

Hi God, it's me.

Today felt light.

Not perfect.

Not without its worries.

Just light.

And that's enough.

Dear God, thank You for the peace that comes when I stop trying to fix everything and simply enjoy being here.

Thank You so much for the laughter that slips in between the tasks and to-do lists.

Thank You for the grace that meets me in every pause.

Dear God, You keep showing me joy doesn't need a reason.

It just needs room.

So today, I give it space to stay.

I give You praise for the goodness already here.

June 7

Hi God, it's me.

Thank You for the gift of now.

This breath.
This pause.

This moment that shimmers with Your goodness.

I don't have to wait for everything
to be perfect to feel peace or joy.

You are here.

In the imperfect.
In the in-between.

In the quiet rhythm of being alive.

Let me live fully today.

Not distracted.
Not distant.

But awake.

Celebrating the wonder of just being.

You meet me in this moment,
and this moment is sacred.

Joy is here too, and I thank You for it.

June 8

Hi God, it's me.

Today I woke up smiling.

Not because everything is easy,
but because I feel You near.

There's a lightness in knowing that I don't walk alone.
That even simple mornings can hold something holy.

Thank You, God,
for the laughter that comes unexpectedly;
for music playing somewhere in the distance;
for small joys that remind me life is still good.

Dear God, please let my heart
stay open to moments like these,
where peace lingers and joy is effortless.

Every time
I notice goodness,
I'm really noticing You.

And that, God, is worth celebrating.

June 9

Hi God, it's me.

Joy met me
in the middle
of an ordinary day.

No big reason.
No special occasion.

Just a moment
that felt full of You.

The peace that followed when I stopped rushing.
The way sunlight poured through the window.
The sound of laughter in another room.

Dear God, thank You for filling
my life with reasons to smile
I didn't have to search for.

Every
moment I notice You
is its own celebration.

Joy isn't far away.
It's already here.

And today, I choose to live in it.

June 10

Hi God, it's me.

I felt
joy rise up today
for no reason at all.

It came quietly,
like a soft song in my spirit,
reminding me that Your presence
is enough to make my heart light.

Dear God, thank You
for days that don't need fixing and
for moments that simply feel right.

Thank You
for the way peace settles in when
I stop trying to control what's next.

You are the joy that steadies me.

The calm beneath the noise.
The reason my soul can sing.

Dear God, my gratitude
is my celebration today.

Every breath of thanks
is its own kind of
hallelujah.

June 11

Hi God, it's me.

Today, I felt surrounded
by small reminders
of Your love.

A smile from a stranger.
A breeze that felt like grace.

A moment of peace
I didn't even ask for.

You find the sweetest
ways to say, *I'm here.*

Dear God, thank You for joy that
meets me where I least expect it.

Thank You for beauty that slips into
ordinary hours and turns them holy.

Let joy linger, dear God.

Let it ripple through everything I do,
so that even my quiet moments
sing back to You.

June 12

Hi God, it's me.

Today, I was reminded how
joy grows when it's shared.

A kind word.
A warm hug.

A moment of laughter that
made the room feel lighter.

You have a way of weaving hearts
together through the simplest things.

Dear God, thank You for the people
who carry Your light so effortlessly.

I thank You
for the joy that passes
from one soul to another.

Such a blessing!

Help me be that kind of presence too.

The kind that lifts, encourages, and
reflects Your love without trying.

Joy shared is joy multiplied.
The sound of Heaven on earth.

June 13

Hi God, it's me.

I woke up today and
joy met me at the door.

It didn't ask for anything.

It just arrived with the sunrise.

The air felt softer.
The world felt kind.

And my heart remembered
how it feels to be held by You.

Oh, Lovely God, thank You
for mornings that whisper promise; and
for peace that settles in like light after rain.

You're
the melody
behind every smile.

The reason my soul can sing.

My joy today is an offering, God.

A simple song of love rising back to You.

June 14

Hi God, it's me.

Today I felt laughter rise
from somewhere deep inside.

The kind of laughter
that doesn't need a reason.

It felt like sunlight in motion, like my spirit
remembering what freedom feels like.

You have such a beautiful way
of bringing joy back to life.

A sacred way of turning
even my stillness
into dance.

Oh, Lovely God!

Thank You for the spark You placed in me; and
for reminding me that celebration is not a moment.

It's a way of being.

Let everything I do today
echo that joy, dear God.

Let it ripple smoothly through
my thoughts, my words, my actions, my smile,
my breath, until the whole day feels like praise.

June 15

Hi God, it's me.

There are moments when
Your goodness stops me in my tracks.

Moments when I look around and
realize how far You've brought me.

How much You've carried.
How gently You've healed.

It overwhelms me, God.

In the best way.

Joy rushes in like
a wave of remembrance.

Not because life is perfect,
but because You've been faithful.

Dear God, thank You for the miracles
that hide daily in Your perfect grace
and for the strength I didn't know
I had until You called it forward.

Oh, Faithful God!

Let gratitude rise like morning light and
fill every corner of my heart with praise.

June 16

Hi God, it's me.

Today I slowed down
and felt joy in the silence.

No music.
No noise.

Just breath and being.

It was enough.

There's a calm that comes when I stop
searching for more and simply sit with You.

Thank You for the still moments that steady my soul.
For peace that hums softly beneath the rush of life.

In the quiet,
I felt Your nearness
wrap around me like light.

And in that moment, I realized,
rest is also a way to praise You.

June 17

Hi God, it's me.

Today I feel
energy in my spirit.

A pull toward life,
toward laughter,
toward light.

Maybe
it's You breathing
something new into me.

A reminder that joy
was never meant to sit still.

God, thank You for every reason to move,
to dance, to lift my head toward the sky
and remember who made it glorious.

You fill the air with possibility.
You fill my heart with songs.

My steps march to Your rhythm.

A quiet dance of gratitude
that keeps leading me
back to You.

June 18

Hi God, it's me.

Sometimes joy
catches me off guard.

It slips in quietly,
like wonder finding
its way home.

I'll see a sky painted with color, or hear a laugh that feels
like music, and suddenly I remember You made all of this.

The beauty.
The breath.

The miracle of being here.

Dear God, I thank You for the way *awe* awakens me.
For turning small moments into glimpses of eternity.

My gratitude rise
like a song You can hear.

Soft and sincere.

Born from the joy
of simply knowing
You.

June 19

Hi God, it's me.

I see joy reflected
in the people around me.

In laughter that fills the room.
In voices overlapping like music.

In the way love feels
lighter when it's shared.

You created us to need one another,
to find You in kindness, in conversations,
and in the simple act of being together.

Dear God, thank You
for community that heals.

For smiles that soften the day.
For connections that feel holy.

Let
my presence bring
light too, dear God.

Let me be the reason
someone remembers
joy today.

June 20

Hi God, it's me.

Today I feel joy
in simply being myself.

Not trying to prove.
Not trying to please.

Just being.

You made me this way on purpose.

Every detail.
Every dream.

Every part of me that carries Your light.

Thank You for teaching
me joy begins within.

God, let my confidence
be quiet but full of truth.

Let it shine softly
as a reflection
of You.

Joy becomes radiant
when it reminds me
of You.

June 21

Hi God, it's me.

The world feels alive today.

The sky looks like worship.

The wind carries whispers of grace.

Everything around me
seems to be singing
Your name.

And for a moment,
I join in without trying.

Dear God, thank You
for beauty that humbles me.

For color, for light, for the language
of creation that speaks without words.

You didn't have to make it this lovely.

But You did.

And every time I notice it,
I feel You smiling through it all.

My *awe* is my offering today, dear God.

Joy is the echo of being deeply loved by You.

June 22

Hi God, it's me.

I didn't realize how heavy my heart
had been until joy found its way back in.

It came gently, like sunlight through clouds, reminding
me gently that healing doesn't always announce itself.

Sometimes, it just begins.

Thank You, God,
for meeting me in the middle
of what once felt impossible.

For proving, again and again,
that sorrow never gets
the final word.

You turn endings into openings.
You turn pain into praise.

And here I am, dear God.

Breathing easier, smiling again.

Remembering how good it feels to be alive.

June 23

Hi God, it's me.

Today my heart feels full.

So full it spills over into laughter, into gratitude,
into the kind of joy that doesn't need explaining.

You've been so good to me.

Even in ways I didn't recognize.

I thank You for the blessings that keep finding me.
And for the grace that multiplies the more I notice it.

I don't want to rush past this feeling, God.

I want to linger here.

In the warmth of Your goodness.
In the rhythm of praise.

Joy is holy.

It's the sound of my soul celebrating You.

June 24

Hi God, it's me.

Today feels calm,
like joy has settled
into peace.

No fireworks.
No rush.

Just stillness
that feels full and holy.

Maybe this is what contentment is.
Not needing more to feel complete.

Thank You, God, for this steady happiness, for this quiet glow within me that doesn't fade when the noise does.

You've taught me
joy doesn't always dance.

Sometimes, it simply stays.

I'm grateful for how it stays, God. For how it rests with me like light that never leaves.

June 25

Hi God, it's me.

Today, I thought about the
people You've placed in my life.

The ones who make me laugh until my cheeks hurt.
The ones who listen when I can't find the words.
The ones who remind me what love feels like.

Thank You for every soul that carries a piece of Your heart.
For the joy that multiplies when we choose to care deeply.

Dear God, You've shown me
we don't walk this road alone.

People are a gift too holy to overlook.

Dear God,
let me cherish them,
let me love them well.

Because joy shared with others
always finds its way back to You.

June 26

Hi God, it's me.

Today I felt peace
in simply letting go.

The urge to fix.
The need to know.
The weight of what-ifs.

I placed it all in Your hands.

And joy met me there.

It wasn't loud or rushed.

Just a quiet gladness that came
from trusting You completely.

Thank You for reminding me
surrender isn't giving up.

It's giving over.

It's remembering I was never
meant to carry anything alone.

Let my faith stay light.
Let my heart stay open.

God, let my joy stay rooted
in the certainty of Your care.

June 27

Hi God, it's me.

I've been thinking
about where I've been.

The prayers I whispered.
The seasons I barely understood.

The moments I thought
I wouldn't make it through.

And yet, here I am.

Still standing.
Still smiling.
Still Yours.

Thank You for every chapter that led me here, God.
For the joy that bloomed in places I once called broken.
For the strength that grew while I was waiting for answers.

You've been my constant, God.
My reason to keep believing.

All I can see is grace.

Grace.

Grace upon grace upon grace.

And joy, quietly rising from the heart of it all.

June 28

Hi God, it's me.

Today I just feel grateful.

Not for what's coming,
not for what's gone,
but for *right now.*

This breath.
This peace.

This sacred middle where
joy feels steady and alive.

You've been with me
through every rise and fall.

And now I see.

Your goodness was never
waiting at the finish line.

It's been here all along.

Thank You for teaching me that presence is its own kind of miracle. That celebration lives in the here and now.

Keep my spirit tender, dear God.

Let this moment stretch into eternity where gratitude becomes worship, and joy becomes communion with You.

June 29

Hi God, it's me.

I can feel
the stillness of the month winding down,
the soft exhale after so many holy moments.

Joy has been my teacher.

It's shown me how light can linger even after the rain.
How laughter can rise from places once filled with tears.

Thank You for showing me joy was never fragile.
It was sacred strength woven through every day.

You've been so faithful, God.

So near.
So kind.
So loving.

Dear God, please let my heart stay open to this quiet wonder.
To the grace that keeps unfolding even when I'm not looking.

As June
fades into memory,
my life keeps singing
the song it taught me:

praise in every breath, joy in every season.

June 30

Hi God, it's me.

What a month it's been!

A chorus of laughter.

Stillness.
Grace.

Grace upon grace upon grace.

You've taught me
joy isn't a fleeting feeling.

It's a way of seeing. A way of being. A quiet,
steady *yes* to the goodness You've already given.

Thank You for every breath that turned into praise and
for every moment that reminded me how alive I am in You.

As June closes, let celebration stay near.

Let it hum beneath my days, a sacred rhythm that never fades.
And when I step into tomorrow, may I carry this truth with me.

Joy was never something I found.

It was You, finding me.

JULY

Freedom & Courage

Freedom is the breath of the soul unbound.

It's the quiet exhale you didn't know you were holding, the sacred release that comes when you stop fighting for control and start trusting the One who holds it all. This month is a call to let go, to loosen your grip on fear, shame, and every weight that keeps you small. It's a month to remember that God has never asked you to carry what was meant to be surrendered.

July invites you to open your hands so heaven can open its doors.

God did not create you to live confined. He created you to live free. Freedom is not the absence of struggle; but the courage to keep walking through it with faith, believing that your steps are guided even when the path feels unclear. It's the quiet bravery to say, I choose peace, even here, even now.

Every act of surrender is a step into holy ground. When you release what no longer serves your becoming, God fills that empty space with His healing presence, His steady assurance, His unwavering love. He fills it with a peace that teaches your spirit to rest and a grace that teaches your heart to rise.

You are stronger than you think.

But even strength bends before grace.

True courage isn't loud. It's the steady heartbeat that whispers, I will not give up. It's the willingness to believe in what God is shaping within you long before you can see it. It's trusting that even when the chains fall slowly, they are still falling; and trusting that God is breaking what once broke you.

Let this month be your turning point. Stand tall in your truth. Lift your face toward the light. Walk forward, not in the absence of fear, but in the presence of faith that carries you further than your feet ever could.

And as you move through July, may you feel heaven surrounding you with gentleness, reminding you that freedom is not something you strive for, but something you step into, little by little, breath by breath. Every moment of release draws you deeper into the life God has written for you, a life where your soul expands, your heart softens, and your spirit remembers its strength.

God's Spirit abides in you.

It is fierce, fearless, and free.

July 1

Hi God, it's me.

A new month is here.
I feel something stirring.

I'm ready to stop living small.
To stop hiding behind fear.
To stop holding back.

I want to walk in freedom.

Not just spiritually.

But emotionally and mentally.

God, show me the places where I've settled.

The lies I've believed.
The chains I've called comfort.
The wounds I've called endurance.

I want to be brave with You, God.

Even if I tremble.
Even if I move slowly.

I want to move forward in freedom with You.

July 2

Hi God, it's me.

Sometimes, I feel stuck
in patterns I didn't choose.

Ways of coping.
Ways of thinking.

Ways of protecting myself
that are no longer serving me.

I don't want to stay trapped in
what I was never meant to carry.

You are the God who sets people free.

So start with me.

Unwind the lies.
Break the cycles.

Loosen the grip of anything
that keeps me from healing.

I want to live whole.
Not just functioning.

Break me open, if You must, dear God.

Set me free with Your love.

July 3

Hi God, it's me.

There are things I've buried.

Fears I dressed up as confidence.
Wounds I covered with pride.
Pain I learned to ignore.

God, You see it.

All of it.

You're not afraid of the mess.

I want to be brave enough to face it with You.
To stop pretending. To stop pushing it down.
To stop calling survival *freedom*.

True healing takes courage.
God, I need courage now.

Walk me through the fire.

God, please don't let me walk alone.

Be with me through the fear, the pain,
the depression, the anxiety, the healing.

Be with me through the love of You and of me too.

July 4

Hi God, it's me.

I'm thinking about the
freedom only You can give.

Freedom from shame.
Freedom from striving.

Freedom from needing
to be someone I'm not.

Let me walk in that today. Let me believe
I'm no longer bound to who I used to be.

I don't have to keep carrying
what You already set me free from.

I'm not waiting for permission.

You already gave it.

Your love unlocked the chains.
Your mercy opened the door.

Now I stand in the light of what You've already done.
Heart lifted, hands open, soul at rest in You.

This is holy ground. This is freedom.
This is grace becoming breath.

July 5

Hi God, it's me.

I don't feel strong today.

I feel unsure.

Tired.

A little bit fragile.

I've been wondering maybe courage
doesn't always look like bold declarations.

Maybe it looks like taking one
step when your legs are shaking.

So I'm stepping anyway.

Into honesty. Into healing.
Into the life You've called me to live.

Walk with me through the fear
and turn it into trust and faith.

Dear God, I know You're shaping
me in the silence and the strain.

Every trembling step becomes a prayer.
Every breath, a hymn of surrender.

In You, even fragility is holy.

July 6

Hi God, it's me.

There's a version of me
I've been afraid to become.

Too loud.
Too wild.
Too honest.

Just way too much.

But maybe that version of me
is the one You created from the start.

The one who speaks truth.

Loves big.
Stands tall.

Doesn't apologize for existing.

I want to meet the unchained version of me. I want to
walk in my shoes without fear, without shrinking my light.

Let me be free enough to fully be myself.
Give me the courage to be who You created.

Shape my boldness with grace.
God, anchor my truth in love.

May my life reflect Your light in every
word, every breath, every becoming.

July 7

Hi God, it's me.

Courage isn't always loud.

Sometimes, it's sitting with
pain instead of running from it.

Sometimes, it's asking for help.

Sometimes, it's choosing joy
when I don't feel ready to celebrate.

God, thank You for giving me
courage that grows slowly.

Not with force.
But with love.

Let me keep showing up as someone
who knows they've already been set free.

Because You did that for me.

God, my freedom honors You.
My courage sings of Your love.

Even when I tremble, my lips still whisper:

You are near.
You are good.
You are everything.

July 8

Hi God, it's me.

I've been carrying things
that don't belong to me.

Expectations. Old guilt. Generational
weight that was never mine to hold.

I'm tired.

I want to lay it down.

Please teach me how to release it.

Not just once, but over and over
until it no longer feels familiar.

I wasn't born to carry every burden.

I was born to walk in truth.
To rise. To love. To live free.

God, please show me how to lay it
all down without reaching for it again.

Release isn't losing.

It's returning.

To peace. To presence. To You.

July 9

Hi God, it's me.

I've been so afraid to let go.

Part of me believes if I release the memory,
the hurt, the story, I'll lose a part of myself.

Maybe that version of me was never meant to last.
Maybe letting go is what makes space for something new.

So I give it to You.

Not because I feel ready, but because
I trust You'll hold it better than I have.

God, free me from what no longer fits.

Take what was heavy and trade it for peace.
Take what was broken and turn it into grace.

Hold what I've outgrown with mercy.
Heal what I've been afraid to release.

And as I let go, let me fall softly into Your peace.

July 10

Hi God, it's me.

Today I choose to stop
apologizing for who I truly am.

For the space I take up. For the
way I speak, feel, glow, and shine.

I'm done shrinking to make
other people comfortable.

You didn't create me to fit in.
You created me to reflect You.

So let me
walk in that identity
with courage and grace.

Not with pride.

But with deep, rooted confidence
that comes from being Yours.

No more hiding.
No more fear.

Only the truth of who I am.

Your reflection.
Your creation.

Your love alive in me.

July 11

Hi God, it's me.

Sometimes healing feels like breaking.
Like I'm losing pieces of myself when really
I'm just shedding what was never meant to stay.

Dear God, be with me in the
breaking and in the unraveling.

Be with me in the moments where I can't tell if I'm
falling apart and breaking or falling freely to safety.

Only You know the difference, Sweet, Precious God.

You know how to hold me
and keep me safe in all things.

Let this healing run deep, God.

I won't rush it.

I'll rest in the slow mercy of Your timing.

Hold me steady.

Until the breaking becomes beauty.
And every wound learns how to worship again.

July 12

Hi God, it's me.

I've been afraid of rejection.

Afraid
that if I show up fully,
someone will turn away.

But You never do.

You stay.

You see every part of
me and love me still.

That kind of love gives me courage.
It reminds me I don't need to earn belonging.

I already belong.

Help me walk in that truth today.

Let it echo in every word I speak.
Let it be the ground I stand on.

When fear starts to whisper in my ears, Sweet Loving God,
remind me to profess boldly that fear has no power over me,
that Your love has already claimed me as Yours.

In that truth, my soul rests.

Safe, seen, and at home with You.

July 13

Hi God, it's me.

Sometimes, I wonder if I'm truly free.

Have I released the past? Or simply
learned how to live around its weight.

I don't want to just survive.

I want to be healed. I want to breathe
again without the ache beneath my ribs.

Dear God, take me deeper.

Not to rearrange my pain.
But to redeem it.

Search my heart where shadows still linger.
Unravel every knot I've tried to hide behind strength.

I don't want to pretend I'm okay.
I want to be made new.

Set me free, Lord.

Not just from what hurt me, but from
the parts of me that learned to hold it.

When the weight begins to lift, let my soul rise too.

Quietly, wholly, into Your light.

July 14

Hi God, it's me.

I've been thinking about
the weight that runs in families.

The fears.
The silence.

The patterns we carry
without even realizing it.

You are a chain-breaker.

And You placed me here to do
things differently for Your glory.

Oh Great, Loving, Powerful God,
help me release what doesn't belong.

Not with anger.
But with grace.

With courage.

With love for where I come from,
and boldness for where I'm going.

Your grace moves through me, turning old
wounds into wisdom, and every chain into light.

Healing flows backward and forward
through generations seen and unseen,
until all that remains is love.

July 15

Hi God, it's me.

I used to think
freedom was a
destination.

Somewhere I'd arrive
when I finally got it right.

But now I see it's a daily decision.

To release.
To remember.

To walk forward
even when I'm afraid.

Thank You for reminding me that I don't
have to wait until I feel ready to live free.

Freedom starts with truth.

And the truth is
I'm already Yours.

So let every breath be a song of release.
And every step a testament to Your grace.

July 16

Hi God, it's me.

I keep waiting for the fear to leave.
But maybe courage isn't about waiting.

Maybe it's about trusting You
enough to move while it's still there.

So today, I won't let fear decide what I do.

I'll take the risk.

Start the thing.
Speak the truth.
Show up fully.

Even if fear rides along, You're the one driving.

Let my faith be louder, God.

Louder than the doubts.
Louder than the fear.

My heart stays tuned to the sound of Your voice.

Steady and sure, calling me forward.

And when the noise fades, only one thing remains.

The still, sacred echo of trust in You.

July 17

Hi God, it's me.

Sometimes freedom feels unfamiliar.

My soul is still learning how
to breathe without the weight.

I've grown so used to heaviness that peace feels foreign.
But just because I carried it doesn't mean I'm meant to keep it.

Teach me the grace of lightness, Lord.

Joy without guilt.
Peace that lingers.
Rest that feels like home.

Keep my hands open when old burdens call my name.
Remind me not to reach for what You've already lifted.

I'm no longer bound.
I'm becoming free.

My heart grows fluent in the language of Your peace.
Breathing in Your presence, resting in Your light.

And remembering
with every breath,
freedom is holy.

July 18

Hi God, it's me.

I want to be brave in the small ways too.

Not just when the stakes are high.
But in the quiet, ordinary moments.

Give me courage to tell the truth softly.

To speak with kindness.

To say *yes* when I'm afraid, and *no* when I need to.

Let freedom live in my choices, not only in
what I've released, but in how I walk forward.

With grace.
With wisdom.
With You.

Teach me that bravery can sound like peace.
That every gentle act of faith is holy in Your eyes.

When my courage feels small,
walk beside me in stillness.

Dear God, my steps find rhythm in Your presence.
Peace becomes my way. Love becomes my strength.

July 19

Hi God, it's me.

Thank You for how far
You've brought me.

Sometimes I forget to pause
and celebrate the distance.

The valleys crossed,
the weight I no longer carry,
the peace that slowly replaced the ache.

Let me take a quiet moment to notice the change. To honor
the healing that happened little by little, grace by grace.

Dear God, thank You
for the strength I didn't know
I held until You called it forward.

Freedom didn't come in an instant.

It came in steps.

In surrender.
In trust. In faith.
In Your steady presence.

And through it all, You were here;
guiding, keeping, loving me home.

And still, You are here.

July 20

Hi God, it's me.

There's a boldness rising in me.

Not loud. Not reckless.
But steady and sure.

Rooted in who You are
and who You say I am.

I don't need to convince anyone.
I don't need to prove anything.

I just need to stay with You.

Let my courage be calm.
Let my words carry truth.
Let my heart stay anchored.

You make me brave, God.

Brave enough to surrender.
Brave enough to simply be.

Your strength becomes my stillness.
Your presence, the place I stand.

July 21

Hi God, it's me.

Freedom isn't only about letting go.

It's about walking differently now.

Moving with grace where chains once were.

Remind me of that today, Lord.

When old thoughts return,
when fear comes knocking,
when comfort calls me back to
what no longer serves my soul.

Teach me to walk as one already delivered.

Empowered by mercy.
Surrounded by love.

My steps remember the sound of release.

My heart stays anchored
in the truth of who I am:

redeemed, restored, free.

Dear God, every step is a prayer of freedom; a quiet hymn of gratitude for all You've set me free from.

July 22

Hi God, it's me.

There's
a quiet strength
rising within me.

The kind that doesn't shout,
but stands tall even while trembling.

I once thought freedom would
sound like thunder, wild and loud.

Now I know it also feels like calm; like peace
that holds steady when everything else sways.

God,
thank You for shaping
me from the inside out.

Thank You for teaching me that
courage can whisper and still be holy.

What You're building in me
isn't loud, but it's lasting.

God, please let me thrive from Your strength.
Rooted in Your peace, anchored in Your love.

The stillness within me
is a mirror of Your grace.

A resting place for Your light to dwell.

July 23

Hi God, it's me.

I've carried fear for so long, I almost forgot what it feels like to walk without it, to live without it.

You're teaching me how to move in faith instead.

Not reckless.
Not perfect.

Just rooted in the truth that You're with me.

I am no longer a prisoner to fear.
My decisions flow from freedom.

Not fear.

Freedom. Freedom. Freedom.

My words rise from truth.

Not insecurity.

This is what courage looks like.
Quiet, steady, holy in its becoming.

As I trust You, every step I take echo this truth:

I am free.
I am safe.
I am Yours.

July 24

Hi God, it's me.

I still have moments when I question myself,
when doubt whispers and confidence fades.

I wonder if I'm enough, if I'm equipped,
if I can truly live what You've placed within me.

But You remind me gently:

I don't need to know
everything to walk in Your light.

I just need to keep saying *yes*.

Yes to growth.
Yes to grace.
Yes to love.

Yes to the version of me that You already see:

whole, capable, becoming.

God, thank You for seeing beyond my hesitation and calling me.
My *yes* is sacred, a quiet echo of trust that reaches Heaven.

It rises like prayer.
Soft but certain.

A vow of love to the One who called me first.

July 25

Hi God, it's me.

I've been letting too many
voices speak louder than Yours.

The weight of opinions,
the booming echoes of regret,
the whispers of my own doubt.

I want to lean in closer to what You say.

You call me chosen.

Free.
Loved.
Capable.
Empowered.

So I will build my heart on Your words alone.

When fear rises, when I feel unsure, please
teach me to return to the sound of Your truth.

Steady, gentle, unchanging.

Your voice is the one that anchors me.
Your love is the quiet where I abide.

With every breath, my soul whispers amen; a quiet prayer
of truth and love, singing softly to praise the Holy One.

July 26

Hi God, it's me.

It takes courage
to keep showing up
and to keep on going.

It takes courage to keep
believing when the path feels heavy,
and the promise still slowly unfolding.

But here I am, Lord.
I haven't turned away.

You never promised ease.
You promised Yourself.

You've kept Your promise in every breath and in every
quiet moment when I thought I was abandoned and alone.

So I will keep walking.

Not because it's effortless.
But because You are near.

Your faithfulness is the rhythm beneath my steps.
Your love is the light that steadies my heart.

When I grow weary, dear God,
let me rest in the quiet certainty of You,
where striving ends and only grace remains.

July 27

Hi God, it's me.

You've been working in silence. Quietly
reshaping what I could not name or notice.

Somewhere in that stillness, peace
began to bloom where fear once lived.

I feel myself changing.

I move slower now.

Surer.

More rooted in the quiet strength of Your mercy.

This freedom isn't loud.

It isn't sudden.

It unfolds the way morning light does:

gently, faithfully.

Every calm breath reminds me You are near.
Every soft surrender is a hymn of becoming.

All that I am,
all I'm still learning to be,
is my offering back to You.

July 28

Hi God, it's me.

You move in ways I can't always see.

I'm learning to trust
the spaces in between the waiting,
the unfolding, the gentle pace of grace.

Not every season asks me to run.

Some ask me to rest.

To listen.

To believe stillness is not delay, but design.

So I'll breathe here awhile, in the quiet of Your timing,
where nothing is wasted and everything is becoming.

Dear God, teach my heart
to move in rhythm with Yours:

unhurried, unafraid, at peace.

July 29

Hi God, it's me.

Freedom doesn't mean
I'll never feel the pull
of old pain.

It means I no longer live there.

When fear tries to return,
when old wounds whisper,
I know how to breathe again.

I know how to listen for Your
voice instead of my own doubt.

Thank You for teaching me how to choose peace.
For showing me how to rise gently each time I fall.

This is freedom.

Not the absence of struggle,
but the grace to keep moving:

in love, in truth, in You.

July 30

Hi God, it's me.

Let me be bold with love today.

Not just brave in what I say.
But brave in how I care.

Brave in how I forgive.
How I show up for others.

Sometimes, the most courageous thing is keeping my heart open in a world that tells me to close it.

You didn't make me hard.

You made me strong.
You made me soft.

You made me
sweet and gentle.

So I'll lead with love.

As You do.
As You are.

As You've created me to be in Your image.

As I am.

July 31

Hi God, it's me.

This month has taught me
what it means to be free.

Not perfect.
Not fearless.

But free.

I've let go.
I've stood up.
I've walked forward.

I refuse to go back.

Let this be a line in the sand.
A commitment to courage.
A declaration of freedom.

I'm no longer bound
to the scared and frail
person I used to be.

I am free.

AUGUST

Trust & Faith

Trust is the stillness before faith takes root, the holy breath before the next becoming. It's the quiet pause where you gently unclench your hands, release what you cannot shape, and lean into the unseen goodness of God. This month invites you to rest in that surrender. To let your spirit exhale. To remember trust is not weakness, but a returning to the One who has never left you.

Faith begins where understanding ends. It rises softly in the dim places, blooming in the very spaces where certainty slips away.

Even when you can't trace the path, God's hand is still guiding what your eyes cannot yet discern. The waiting is not wasted. It's sacred ground, the soil where deeper trust grows. Every unanswered prayer, every quiet ache, every moment of silence is a holy exchange between your heart and God.

You don't have to make sense of everything. You don't have to gather every piece or predict what's coming. God is already holding what feels too heavy for you to lift. Your only work is to stay open, to breathe through the tenderness of the unknown, and to let your heart believe that His timing is not just perfect. It's personal. God's timing is shaped with you in mind.

Choose to stand in faith even when you can't feel God's nearness. Choose to trust Him even when His steps are hidden, even when the night feels long. The miracle is already unfolding in ways you cannot yet recognize. The light is already on its way toward you, preparing to meet you with more grace than you expect.

This is the sacred strength of August: a month carved out for trust, for faith, for resting in the arms of the God who holds what you fear, heals what you hide, and guides you toward what He has lovingly prepared.

Before you step into the days ahead, pause here in this holy beginning. Let August open gently within you like a whispered invitation from God. Allow trust to steady your breath and faith to soften your gaze. Stand in this sacred threshold knowing that you are guided, guarded, and gracefully led. God goes before you. God walks beside you. God is already preparing the miracle your heart has been yearning for.

August 1

Hi God, it's me.

A new month begins.
I place it in Your hands.

I don't know what waits ahead.
But I know who goes with me.

Teach me to trust without needing proof.
Teach me to believe without demanding signs.

Let
faith be my rhythm,
and trust be my rest.

When the path feels hidden,
let my heart remember
You're already there.

Dear God,
anchor my soul
in Your promise.

Holy Father, let my life become
an echo of Your unseen grace.

August 2

Hi God, it's me.

I've spent so much time second-guessing myself.

Overplanning.
Overthinking.
Overanalyzing.

Trying to do everything right instead of simply trusting You.

So here I am.

Not striving for clarity.
But surrendering to faith.

What do You want me to see today?
Where are You asking me to go?

What's mine to carry?
What must I release into Your hands?

Give me discernment, dear God.

The kind that grows from stillness,
that anchors me when I can't see the next step,
that reminds me You're always leading the way.

Teach me to trust more than I reason, to believe more than I fear. I rest in the truth that Your timing is always perfect.

God, I place my faith in You.

August 3

Hi God, it's me.

Some days feel still.

Almost too still.

I pray.
I wait.
I hope.

Yet, everything looks the same.

But God,
You remind me faith
is not proven by movement.

It's rooted in trust.

When the soil looks dry,
the seeds are still becoming.

When I can't see growth,
You're working beneath the surface.

Teach me to stay faithful in the silence.
To believe delay is not denial.

I find comfort in the unseen rhythm of Your will,
the holy patience that turns waiting into worship.

God, when nothing seems to move,
let my heart remember You are here.

August 4

Hi God, it's me.

Sometimes my plans
crumble right in front of me.

The things I thought were certain
begin to slip through my hands.

And I feel the ache of letting go,
the grief of not knowing
what comes next.

But even here,
You are steady.

You are sure.
You are still good.

God, please help me trust
what I can't yet understand.

Help me believe that what feels
like loss might be love in disguise.

When my plans fall apart, let my faith rise stronger. When the path changes, teach me to see Your hand in the reroute.

God,
make my trust unshakable in the face of the unknown.
Let my faith be my peace when everything else shifts.

August 5

Hi God, it's me.

Waiting is never easy.

My heart wants answers now.
My mind keeps wondering when.

But You keep whispering
not yet doesn't mean never.

You are still aligning.

Still preparing.

Still weaving
things together
in ways I can't yet see.

Please teach me to find peace in the pauses.
Teach me to see the beauty in divine delay.

Patience becomes my prayer
and trust, my resting place.

Your timing is not slow.

It's sacred.

God, please help me wait with faith;
for every moment withheld is filled
with holy purpose and sacred love.

August 6

Hi God, it's me.

There are days when
the way ahead feels hidden.

When the light fades
before I take the next step.

Still, I walk.

Not by sight.

But
by the soft knowing
that You are near.

Faith feels like air sometimes.
Invisible, but enough to breathe.

God,
when uncertainty presses in,
wrap me in Your peace.

Let trust become the
rhythm of my
breath.

You have never failed me.
And I know You never will.

Dear God, even in the mystery, let my
faith stay fierce, and my heart stay still.

August 7

Hi God, it's me.

Sometimes my thoughts grow loud,
and my heart forgets how to listen.

I chase
my own reasoning,
trying to make sense
of what only faith can hold.

But, Your voice!

It comes like a whisper in the wind:

soft, sure, steady.

It doesn't rush.
It doesn't force.

It simply reminds me peace
is proof of Your presence.

Dear God,
please teach me
to follow that peace.

To lean into Your still, small voice even when it
leads me away from what I thought I wanted.

Dear God, quiet my mind until I hear You clearly.
Let trust guide me where understanding cannot.

August 8

Hi God, it's me.

Sometimes
fear finds me
before faith does.

It rushes in uninvited.
Heavy, loud, unrelenting.

Even then, You are near.

You breathe
peace into the panic,
light into the trembling.

When my thoughts spiral,
God, please hold me still.

When my heart races,
remind me it beats
in Your rhythm.

I don't have to fix what I feel.

I only have to rest in the
safety of Your presence.

Dear God, when fear rises, let faith rise higher.
When I forget who I am, remind me whose I am.

Yours.

August 9

Hi God, it's me.

Disappointment has a way
of leaving echoes in the soul.

Dreams I thought were certain
now rest in pieces at Your feet.

And yet, even in the ache of what
didn't unfold, I feel Your nearness.

You're the God who rebuilds
what was never truly lost.

The One who turns endings
into beginnings wrapped in grace.

God, teach me to trust again.

Not because
everything makes sense,
but because You are still good.

I release what I can't repair,
and hold fast to what still lives:

hope, faith, and the promise of Your love.

Dear God, my heart heals gently in Your timing.
My faith blooms again where sorrow once grew.

August 10

Hi God, it's me.

I had a picture in my mind
of how life was supposed to look.

But slowly, You've been
teaching me that Your way
is gentler, truer, wiser than mine.

I don't always understand
why certain doors close,
or why the timing shifts.

You see the whole story.
I only see the page I'm on.

So today, I choose to trust
what I cannot yet comprehend.

To believe every
redirection is protection.
Every delay, divine design.

Dear God, rewrite my desires
until they sound like Your will.

My faith rests easy
in the beauty of Your plan.

August 11

Hi God, it's me.

There are days
when silence
feels heavy.

When prayers linger unanswered, and
I start to wonder if You still see me.

But even in the quiet, You are near.

You are working in whispers and weaving
purpose through what feels like pause.

Remind me that being unseen
doesn't mean being unloved.

Hidden seasons are holy too.

When I feel forgotten,
let faith be my reminder.

You never leave.
You never forget.
You never overlook.

When I cannot feel You,
my lips shout for Your name.

God, my heart believes You are here.

Always.

August 12

Hi God, it's me.

Starting over feels
both sacred and strange.

Like standing on new ground with traces
of what once was still clinging to my feet.

Part of me fears what's ahead.
Part of me aches for what I left behind.

But all of me belongs to You.

You are the God
of new beginnings.

The restorer of what
time thought it could take.

You turn
endings into entrances
and loss into light.

Dear God, please teach me to trust
that I'm not starting from nothing.

I'm starting from grace.

Dear God, walk with me into what's next.
Steady my heart as faith leads me forward.

August 13

Hi God, it's me.

Some days it feels
like nothing is moving.

Like all my prayers are hanging in the air,
waiting for a distant wind to carry them somewhere.

Maybe progress isn't always visible. Maybe it's
the quiet growth taking place beneath the surface.

The unseen becoming
that only You can measure.

God, please remind me when I can't see
the change, that You are still working.

You are still forming something
holy out of what feels unfinished.

God,
help me trust the process
as much as the promise.

May my faith stay rooted
when the harvest hasn't come.

I trust that it will
in Your divine timing.

It always does.

August 14

Hi God, it's me.

You've been growing
something in me.

Not loud.
But deep.

A maturity that doesn't panic.
A trust that doesn't rush.

A faith that stays rooted
when the next step isn't clear.

Thank You for that.

Dear God, thank You for teaching me to listen
before I speak. To pause before I act and react,
and to ask questions before I assume.

That's what trust and faith in You looks like.

I want more of it.

Keep shaping me, God.

Until my life becomes
a quiet reflection of
Your steadiness
and grace.

August 15

Hi God, it's me.

There are prayers
I've prayed more than once.

Whispers
that rise to heaven
and return in silence.

It used to make me wonder if You heard me at all.
But I'm learning gently, silence doesn't mean absence.

It often means You're doing
something deeper than what I asked for.

Dear God, You see the layers I can't.
You guard the timing I don't understand.

In every delay,
You're still delivering love.

So I'll keep trusting, even when heaven feels quiet.
I'll keep believing, even when answers don't appear.

My faith rests not in outcomes.

But in You.

The One who hears.
The One who holds.
The One who knows.

August 16

Hi God, it's me.

You know my heart
better than I do.

Every ache, every hope, every hidden
prayer I've never found the words for.

I've tried to guard it on my own,
to protect it from breaking again.

But sometimes I forget
my heart is safest in Your hands.

You hold what others mishandled. You mend
what I thought would never feel whole again.

God, teach me to trust You with all I feel.
To open my heart without fear of loss.
To love, to forgive, to begin again.

You're the keeper of it all.

Dear God,
make my heart soft but strong,
open but anchored in You.

My heart beats in rhythm
with Your love and light.

August 17

Hi God, it's me.

Love feels different now.

It's quieter.
Holier.

More like surrender than searching.

You've shown me love isn't something I chase.
It's something I become when I let You heal me.

For every place
that once closed in pain,
You've opened space for peace.

For every scar,
You've written mercy.

I'm learning to love again.

Not from fear of being alone.

But from the fullness of being known by You.

God, let my love reflect Yours.
Patient, kind, anchored in truth.

Every heartbeat is a quiet hallelujah
for the way You make all things new.

August 18

Hi God, it's me.

Trusting myself with people
is one of the hardest things to do.

My heart
wants to hide, to understand.
To fix what only You can heal.

You keep reminding me love is
safest when it rests in Your will.

Teach me to trust, God, that You know who belongs
in my life and who is only meant to pass through.

Teach me to believe that release can be holy too.

When distance grows or silence settles in,
help me not to lose faith in love itself.

You are
still writing stories
I cannot yet see.

I place every connection in Your care.
Every friend, every love, every bond.

May I love without fear,
and let go without bitterness.

God, whoever is meant to stay
in my life, will stay through You.

August 19

Hi God, it's me.

Sometimes
the future feels way too far
to reach and too unclear to see.

It's not mine to control.
It's Yours to unfold.

God, You see the chapters I can't.
You hold the details my heart
keeps trying to plan.

I'm choosing to rest in the grace of not knowing.
I faithfully trust that every step ahead is already
covered by Your goodness.

God, when fear of the unknown creeps in,
remind me that faith was made for this.

For walking on what I can't yet see.
For believing You're already there.

Dear God, write my future with Your wisdom.
Guide it with Your love. Anchor it with Your peace.

Take the pen and write what's best.

Dear God,
let my life unfold as a
reflection of Your perfect will.

August 20

Hi God, it's me.

Sometimes, life unravels
quickly without warning.

What once felt certain suddenly slips away.
And in that breaking, I feel both loss and invitation.

To trust You deeper.
To believe You're still here.

You've never promised things would always stay the same.
What You've promised is to always remain by my side.

When the plans fall apart,
let my faith fall into You.

Dear God, when the pieces scatter,
teach me to see beauty in the undoing.

Because maybe this too is part of Your making.

God, when I cannot hold it all together,
hold me, hold me, hold me, hold me.

Hold me, dear God.

Be my surrender.
Be my strength.

August 21

Hi God, it's me.

You never waste what breaks.

The pieces I thought were ruined
become part of Your redemption.

You rebuild slowly, carefully;
an artist restoring something sacred.

Though I can't always see what You're
creating, I feel Your grace in the process.

Soft, steady, sure.

You take
what shattered in my hands
and make it whole in Yours.

Not as it was, but as it was meant to be.

God, teach me to trust Your timing
as You rebuild what I surrendered.

My faith is patient in You.

My heart opens to welcome
the beauty being created
from what once broke.

August 22

Hi God, it's me.

Healing feels different now.
It's softer than I expected.

Quieter too, like peace
settling where pain once lived.

For so long I prayed for the
mending of my wounds.

But now I see!

The miracle was never just the healing.
It was the way You held me through it.

You didn't just fix what was broken.

You renewed who I am.

You turned sorrow into strength,
and taught me joy without striving.

Now that I'm whole again, teach me not to fear the
calm and to trust the goodness that follows the storm.

My healing honors You.

My peace is proof that You are still faithful.
My life is a testimony of all You've restored.

August 23

Hi God, it's me.

Change always finds
me before I feel ready.

It asks me to release what's
known and step into what's new.

But You, God,
You remain the same.

Constant. Steady.

Unmoved by what shifts around me.

When life rearranges itself, help
me remember transition isn't loss.

It's transformation.

You're simply moving me
from comfort to calling.

From what was to what will be.

Faith is my footing when everything else feels unsteady.
Trust is my anchor as I walk into what I can't yet name.

Holy Father God, my heart becomes brave in the
becoming, every change drawing me closer to You.

August 24

Hi God, it's me.

Some dreams feel
too big for my hands.

Too sacred to rush.
Too fragile to carry alone.

I know
You placed them
in me for a reason.

They are not accidents.

They're seeds of purpose
waiting for Your timing to bloom.

When I grow impatient, remind me faith is the soil where dreams take root; trust is the water that keeps them alive.

I don't want to build without You.

I don't want to force what You're still forming.

Dear God,
teach me to hold my dreams gently,
to believe in what I can't yet see.

I rest in the truth that
what comes from You
will never pass me by.

August 25

Hi God, it's me.

There are lessons I only learned through tears.
Truths that bloomed from the soil of heartbreak.

Though I once wished those seasons
away, I see now they were sacred too.

You were shaping me in the shadows.

Teaching me
how to forgive, how to release,
how to love without losing myself.

The pain wasn't punishment.

It was preparation.

It taught me how to
see You in the breaking.

Dear God,
I trust You with what I've lived through,
with every scar that still remembers.

My healing holds wisdom.
My story carries light.

Nothing is wasted when it's in Your hands.

August 26

Hi God, it's me.

I've tried to plan
my way through life.

To map it out.
To make it make sense.

But
the more I release control,
the more I find peace.

Every time I let go, You show me
Your way is always better than mine.

When I don't understand the turns,
You already see the destination clearly.

When the waiting feels endless,
You're still writing something good.

Today, I place it all in Your hands.

My plans.
My hopes.
My dreams.

I don't need to know how it all unfolds.
I just need to know You're the One unfolding it.

My life is Yours. Lead it, guide it, keep it.
Every breath I take is a quiet act of trust.

August 27

Hi God, it's me.

The month is winding down,
and my heart is getting so full.

You've been teaching me how to trust You in the quiet
and how to believe You when nothing seems sure.

What once made me anxious now feels like peace.
What once felt uncertain now feels like surrender.

You've shown me faith isn't
about having all the answers.

It's about resting in the One who does.

God, thank You for every moment that
stretched my belief and deepened my roots.

Thank You for proving You never leave.

Dear God, as this month begins to close,
my gratitude rises higher than my fears.

My trust remains steady.

My faith continues to grow
in the rhythm of Your love.

August 28

Hi God, it's me.

Thank You for this month and for
every lessons that stretched me.

Thank You for every pause that humbled me.
Every quiet moment that called me closer to You.

I came into August wanting to trust You more.
Somehow, through it all, You made that happen.

You turned uncertainty into peace,
fear into faith, control into surrender.

When I doubted, You stayed steady.
When I wavered, You held me still.

Now I know trust isn't a destination.
It's a daily returning to Your heart.

Holy Father God, I thank You
for teaching me to rest in You.

Keep this faith alive in me,
so that whatever comes next,
my first response will always be trust.

August 29

Hi God, it's me.

This month
has been a quiet
miracle.

You've steadied me
in ways I didn't ask for.

Faith, I'm learning,
isn't about knowing.

It's about trusting that You do.

Through
every rise and fall,
You've been constant.

Through
every silence,
You've been near.

Dear God, thank You
for teaching me that
surrender is holy.

Peace begins where control ends.

August 30

Hi God, it's me.

I've seen
Your hand
in everything.

In the pauses.
In the breakthroughs.

In the moments that didn't
make sense until they did.

You've been patient with me,
teaching me how to trust deeper,
to walk slower, to believe longer.

Thank You for every reminder.

I am held.
I am guided.
I am loved.

August 31

Hi God, it's me.

We've come to
the end of this month.

I can feel the stillness of Your
faithfulness settling all around me.

You've taught me to rest in what I can't control, to trust what
I can't yet see, and to believe Your timing is always perfect.

Every moment,
every pause, every prayer.
You've used it all to draw me closer.

I lay this month before
You with a grateful heart.

Nothing wasted.
Nothing lost.

Only grace upon grace.

God, thank You
for the gift of trust.

Thank You for the strength of faith.
Thank You for never letting go of me.

SEPTEMBER

Wisdom & Discernment

Wisdom begins in stillness, in the quiet places where the heart softens enough to hear. This month invites you to slow your steps, to breathe before you respond, to seek God's whisper before you move forward. September is a sacred pause, a gentle invitation to return to the inner sanctuary where truth rises without force and clarity unfolds without strain.

Discernment is not born from noise. It lives in peace. It grows in the spaces where your soul finally has room to breathe. It's the quiet courage to trust what you feel in your spirit, even when your mind demands evidence. It's the gentle knowing that says, this way, even when reason argues otherwise, even when the path ahead is not yet illuminated.

God's wisdom doesn't rush. It doesn't pressure or push. It arrives softly, through awareness, through alignment, through surrender. It comes like dawn; slow, certain, unavoidable. It doesn't shout for your attention. It settles into your spirit until truth feels unmistakably clear, until peace becomes the compass that points you forward.

The holiest choices are often the ones made in patience, in faith, in quiet trust that God is guiding every step you have yet to take.

Sometimes the most sacred thing you can do is wait. To hold your questions without forcing an answer. To rest in the tension without demanding immediate release. To believe that what feels uncertain now will unfold in its perfect time. Waiting is not weakness. It's worship. It's a declaration that you trust the One who sees beyond what you can comprehend.

You are not alone in your decisions. The same Spirit that hovered over creation now lives within you, breathing wisdom into every anxious corner. You can ask and be guided. You can seek and find. Even when your heart wonders if it can still hear Him, grace ensures you will not miss what is meant for you.

Let this month be your practice of deep listening. Listen beneath fear, beneath distraction, beneath your own reasoning. Listen until your heart steadies, until your spirit softens, until your inner world grows quiet enough to recognize the holy. God is not only speaking to your mind but to your heart. And when the world quiets enough, you will know His voice. When you rest in stillness, wisdom will meet you there, shaping your steps with peace, clarity, and divine discernment.

September 1

Hi God, it's me.

A new month has come. With it,
another chance to lean on your wisdom.

I don't know
what these days will bring,
but I know Who guides me.

Teach me to walk into September
with steady trust and a listening heart.

Not rushing.
Not worrying.

Not clinging to what I can't control.

I want to rest in the quiet knowing
that You already see the way ahead.

Beginnings are sacred ground.
Wisdom often waits in stillness.

I don't have to have every answer
to be held by the One who does.

I open this month with surrender.
I surrender all to You, dear God.

Every thought. Every step. Every outcome.

September 2

Hi God, it's me.

Sometimes, I mistake
my thoughts for Your voice.

God, please teach me to recognize the difference.
To wait for the calm that carries Your presence.

I want to listen for peace.

Not urgency.

Quiet the noise within me.

The questions that rush.
The fears that echo too loud.

Dear God, let discernment
rise like morning light, soft yet certain,
illuminating what confusion once concealed.

Your wisdom is never hurried, never harsh.

It moves through me like breath,
like water finding its way home.

God, please help me.
Help me listen deeply.

I want to feel You
beneath my thoughts, so I can meet You
in the stillness where only faith can see.

September 3

Hi God, it's me.

I'm learning
wisdom isn't loud.

It doesn't rush to speak.
It doesn't need to prove.

Your wisdom listens first.

It feels before it reacts.
It sees what eyes alone can't.

God, teach me to move with that kind of grace,
to think with patience and to discern with peace.

Let wisdom shape my words before they leave my mouth,
and guide all of my thoughts before they take root in fear.

God, fill me with understanding that reflects Your heart:

gentle, steady, sure.

And when I lose my way,
let wisdom be the altar
where I kneel
to find
You.

September 4

Hi God, it's me.

Today I ask for wisdom
that steadies, not sways.

The kind
that doesn't seek to be right,
but is always rooted in truth.

Holy Father God, teach me to see beyond appearances,
to notice what's hidden, to listen for what silence is saying.

Let my heart
become discerning.

Patient enough to wait,
humble enough to learn.

When emotions rise too quickly,
let understanding slow me down.

And when the world pulls for answers, remind me that wisdom often waits in quiet places, growing gently like light after dawn.

September 5

Hi God, it's me.

Thank You for showing me that wisdom
is not only what I know, but how I love.

Your wisdom softens
what pride hardens.

It humbles what ego defends.

It teaches me to respond with grace
when it would be easier to turn away.

God, shape my heart to reflect Yours.

Slow to speak,
quick to understand,
gentle even when it's hard.

Let wisdom
flow through my kindness,
through the patience in my words,
through the peace I carry into a room.

May those who meet me feel the warmth
of Your understanding before I ever say a word.

September 6

Hi God, it's me.

I'm learning
wisdom forgives
what pride remembers.

It doesn't keep score.
It sees through the eyes of grace.
It understands holding on only keeps me bound.

Holy Father God, please teach me to release what hurt me.
Not because it was right, but because freedom lives in letting go.

Forgiveness is not weakness.

It's strength refined by love.

God, soften my heart where it still resists.

Heal the corners of me that cling to what should have passed.
Let mercy become my teacher and compassion my response.

Dear God, breathe Your divine truth
into the quiet chambers of my soul.

Forgiveness abides where Your wisdom dwells.

September 7

Hi God, it's me.

There's a peace
that follows forgiveness.

It doesn't rush in.

It arrives slowly, like dawn
unfolding over quiet waters.

I feel it in the silence where pain once spoke.
In the stillness where resentment used to live.

Your wisdom restores what worry once unraveled.
It reminds me that peace is not found in control.

But in surrender.

Dear God, teach me to guard
this peace as something holy.

To keep it tender.
To keep it true.

Your wisdom is the gentle pulse that
steadies my soul and reminds me:

I am free.

September 8

Hi God, it's me.

Wisdom humbles me in the best ways.

It reminds me that strength is not loud, and confidence does not need to always be seen.

True wisdom stands still.

It listens before it speaks.
It serves without needing praise.

Dear God, please teach me to walk that way.
With quiet assurance. With peace instead of pride.

Let humility
become my posture,
and discernment my crown.

When I'm tempted to prove or perform, whisper to my heart that being grounded in You is enough.

Wisdom doesn't boast.

It simply shines with the calm knowing
that all things begin and end in You.

September 9

Hi God, it's me.

Teach me
the wisdom
of quiet words.

The kind that heals, not harms.
The kind that carries peace, not pride.

God, help me know when to speak
and when silence is the greater truth.

Wisdom reminds me not every
thought needs to be shared.

Not every truth
needs to be told.

Sometimes, love is the pause itself.
The stillness between sentences.

Dear God, let my words
be weighed in gentleness.

Seasoned with grace and mercy,
and guided always by Your Spirit.

When I do not know what to say,
let silence become our shared prayer.

September 10

Hi God, it's me.

Teach
me the patience
that wisdom carries.

The kind that pauses before
deciding and prays before moving.

I don't want to rush ahead of You.
I want to walk in rhythm with Your timing.

God, remind me that waiting is not
wasting, that stillness can be strength.

Peace often speaks before clarity shows up.

When I am tempted to hurry,
slow me with Your presence.

Let discernment rise like calm water after the storm.

And when the answer finally comes,
dear God, let my spirit recognize it.

Not by noise or urgency.

But by the quiet, holy certainty of Your voice.

September 11

Hi God, it's me.

There's wisdom in letting go.

Not from giving up.
But from giving over.

Every plan. Every outcome.
Every need to know how it ends.

Surrender isn't weakness.

It's faith in motion.

It's trust choosing
peace over pressure.

God, teach me to release what was never mine to carry.
To rest my hands so You can move freely through them.

When I loosen my grip,
I make room for grace.

And when I surrender,
I discover that wisdom has been
there all along waiting for me to stop
striving and simply believe You've got me.

September 12

Hi God, it's me.

Sometimes,
faith feels fragile,
like a flame in the wind.

Your wisdom teaches me to protect it.

Not by control.
But by trust.

When I cannot see the way, You remind
me that clarity is not the same as closeness.

I don't have
to understand
to know You're here.

When doubt begins to whisper, let wisdom steady me.
Let it quiet the noise and strengthen my belief that
even in uncertainty, You are guiding every step.

Faith and wisdom walk together.

One believes.
The other sees.

And when I stand
between both,
I find peace.

September 13

Hi God, it's me.

Your wisdom guards
my peace like a gentle shield.

It keeps my mind steady when the world spins too fast.
It reminds me not every storm deserves my attention.

Dear God, teach me to protect
the quiet You've placed within me.

To recognize when worry knocks
and choose prayer instead of panic.

Dear God, let discernment stand at the door of my thoughts,
letting in only what nourishes, what uplifts, what honors You.

And when the noise grows loud,
draw me back to the center
of Your stillness.

God, wrap me in the hush of holy calm,
where peace is not fleeting but eternal.

A sacred resting place within Your heart.

September 14

Hi God, it's me.

Open my eyes to see as wisdom sees.

To look beyond appearances, beyond emotions,
beyond doubt, and find the truth that rests in You.

God, let understanding rise like sunlight, gentle
and certain, showing beauty where fear once lived.

Teach me to see through grace. To notice the small miracles,
the quiet goodness, the sacred patterns You weave each day.

Wisdom is the calm within the storm,
the peace that listens before it speaks,
the light that stays when everything else fades.

It's love
expressed through
understanding.

Wisdom is truth carried in gentleness.
Clarity born from communion with You.

God, when I walk into
wisdom, I walk in joy.

I walk in freedom.
I walk in You.

September 15

Hi God, it's me.

Thank You for the quiet ways
Your wisdom moves through me.

It softens my thoughts, steadies my heart,
brightens my soul, and turns my waiting into peace.

You are
the light behind my understanding,
the calm within my knowing.

I don't have to search far.

You are wisdom itself:
gentle, holy, near.

God, my days reflect what
I've learned in Your presence.

Every choice touched by Your grace.
My life speaks of You without a word.

September 16

Hi God, it's me.

Teach me to live
what wisdom teaches.

Not only to understand.
But to become understanding.

Not only to know love.
But to be love.

Your wisdom moves gently;
lifting, guiding, healing.

Never forcing.
Always flowing.

It shapes the way I listen.

The way I give.
The way I see others.

God, every act of kindness becomes
a reflection of Your heart within mine.

When I embody Your wisdom,
love becomes the clearest sign
You're alive in me.

September 17

Hi God, it's me.

There are moments
when words fall away,
and all that remains is *awe*.

Your presence fills the quiet.

My spirit knows this is wisdom too.

Not the wisdom that thinks.
But the wisdom that kneels.

It's the wisdom that sees
how vast You are and still
I'm safe inside Your light.

I want to shine in this wonder;
to let reverence soften my heart
and gratitude steady my days.

Sacred *awe* is its own kind of knowing.

The kind
that doesn't
need answers.

Only You.

September 18

Hi God, it's me.

Today I feel grateful for the
way wisdom slows me down.

I'm grateful for how it teaches me
to see what I once rushed past.

Your presence is everywhere,
woven through ordinary moments.

In sunlight on my skin.
In laughter I didn't expect.
In the breath that steadies me.

Gratitude opens my eyes
to how near You've always been.
It turns simple moments into sacred ones.

I walk through this day fully awake to wonder.

My thankfulness is its own kind of prayer.

Wisdom is not only knowing.

It's remembering
every good thing
is touched by
You.

September 19

Hi God, it's me.

Some lessons arrive through pain.

Not because You sent it, but
because I chose to learn this way.

Still, You meet me there.

You take what hurts and
turn it into understanding.

Nothing is wasted in Your hands. Even
the ache becomes a seed of becoming.

You never punish.
You reveal.

You never abandon.
You transform.

Through every tear, wisdom takes root.
Through every moment of breaking,
something holy always grows.

Dear God, You use all
things to make me wise.

Pain is not the purpose.

It's the passage through
which love learns to see.

September 20

Hi God, it's me.

Healing has its own wisdom.

It doesn't rush.
It restores.

You take the pieces I once called broken and
show me they were only becoming whole.

Every scar tells a story of how grace
touched pain and turned it into light.

Your wisdom renews
me from the inside out.

Softly.
Quietly.
Completely.

I no longer chase what was lost.

I honor what remains, and I thank You for
what now blooms where sorrow used to live.

Healing is holy.

Wisdom is the gentle hand
that makes all things new.

September 21

Hi God, it's me.

Wisdom
is teaching me to see
through softer eyes.

To look beyond actions and into hearts.
To remember pain wears many faces.

Compassion feels like You.

Gentle, patient,
willing to understand
before being understood.

I no longer need to judge what I can choose to bless.
I no longer need to fix what I can love instead.

When
I see others with grace,
I see You more clearly too.

Wisdom is not only knowing.

It's mercy in motion.
It's love made kind.

September 22

Hi God, it's me.

I noticed Your wisdom teaches balance.
How to open my heart without emptying it.

To give with sincerity, but not from depletion.
To love deeply, but still listen to peace within.

Compassion needs
boundaries to breathe.

Kindness must flow through truth.

I'm learning
that saying no
can also be holy.

Protecting
my peace honors
the love You placed in me.

Wisdom does not pull me apart.

It holds me together.

A harmony of grace and truth,
of open hands and steady ground.

September 23

Hi God, it's me.

Your wisdom lives within me.
A gentle compass, steady and sure.

I used
to doubt the whispers,
second-guess the peace.

Now
I'm learning to trust the sound
of Your stillness inside my soul.

You speak
through intuition, through ease,
through a calm that doesn't compete.

Every time I follow what feels aligned
and true, I find You waiting there.

Self-trust is holy.

It's believing
the wisdom You placed in me
is enough to guide my steps.

And as I listen, I remember:

You are not far.

You are the voice within that knows.

September 24

Hi God, it's me.

Your wisdom gives me confidence.

Not the kind that shouts,
but the kind that stands still.

It doesn't need applause.

It rests in knowing
when I walk with You,
I walk in purpose.

I no longer shrink to make others comfortable.
I no longer question what You've confirmed within me.

Your presence is my courage.
Your peace is my proof.

Each step becomes a declaration:

I am guided.
I am growing.
I am grounded.

In this quiet certainty, I find You again.

The source of all I'm becoming,
the strength behind my stillness,
the light that illuminates my path.

September 25

Hi God, it's me.

Wisdom reminds me
that strength and humility
can live in the same heart.

I can walk boldly
and still bow
softly.

Confidence without grace
is just noise without light.

Dear God, keep my spirit grounded in
gentleness, no matter how high I rise.

Let
my victories speak quietly,
my kindness echo loudly,
my heart stay teachable
even in certainty.

True wisdom does not boast.

It bends toward love.
It kneels in gratitude.

It shines without trying to be seen.

September 26

Hi God, it's me.

Your wisdom teaches me
to be true when no one sees.

To keep my word when it costs me something.
To choose honesty when silence would be easier.

Integrity is quiet.

It carries the sound of peace.

Integrity is doing what's right
even when no one applauds.

Dear God,
You remind me
that character is the altar
where choice becomes worship.

Let
my actions reflect the same
truth my prayers proclaim.

Wisdom is living the light I've been given.

You.

September 27

Hi God, it's me.

Some days feel ordinary.

But I know nothing is wasted with You.

Every task.
Every moment.

Every heartbeat of devotion becomes holy in Your sight.

Your wisdom reminds me faithfulness begins in the little things.
The unseen moments, the quiet choices, the small *yeses*.

They shape who I become.

Consistency is its own kind of worship. A steady
devotion to what You've placed in my hands.

I show up with love in the ordinary,
with excellence in the simple,
with gratitude in the daily.

For it is here,
in the rhythm of repetition,
that wisdom grows roots.

And it is here, in doing the small things well,
that I learn how to honor You in all things.

September 28

Hi God, it's me.

Today wisdom looks like staying.

Not rushing the process.
Not doubting the purpose.

Just standing where You planted me.

Perseverance isn't loud.
It doesn't beg to be seen.

It simply breathes,
one faithful moment at a time.

Your wisdom strengthens me in the waiting,
reminding me growth often happens underground.

When progress feels hidden,
something sacred is forming.

Endurance becomes a prayer.
Patience becomes praise.

And wisdom
keeps whispering,
keeps tending the roots.

The harvest is already on its way.

September 29

Hi God, it's me.

Thank You for the wisdom
You've planted deep
within my soul.

It has steadied me in silence,
guided me through questions,
and softened every corner that
once resisted grace.

I see now how You were
shaping me all along.

Teaching
patience through waiting,
strength through stillness,
understanding through love.

Your timing is perfect.

Nothing arrives too early.
Nothing is ever lost in delay.

This month,
You've taught me to trust the unfolding.
To honor what's growing quietly inside me.

Wisdom has become my rhythm, my rest.
My reminder that everything is right on time.

September 30

Hi God, it's me.

As this month ends,
my heart bows in gratitude.

You've written
wisdom into the rhythm of my days.
In silence and stillness. In lessons and light.

You've shown me wisdom
is not a single moment,
but a way of seeing.

A way of being.
A way of loving.

I carry it forward now.

Not as knowledge.
But as presence.

A calm awareness that You are near in all things.

Thank You for teaching me to listen deeply.

To live gently.
To walk wisely.

I close this month with peace
in my spirit and praise on my lips.

Wisdom has finally come home.

OCTOBER

Surrender & Healing

There's a sacred hush in surrender. It's not the language of loss. It's the language of love. To surrender is to bow the soul, to unclench what was never yours to carry, to lay your pain at the feet of the One who knows how to turn wounds into wisdom.

This month, Heaven whispers to release.

Release what has finished its purpose; the ache that taught you, the control that drained you, the sorrow that sculpted your strength. There's holiness in loosening your grip, in allowing what's heavy to fall away. You don't need to fight every ending or understand every turn. Sometimes healing begins only when you exhale the need to know and simply rest in the arms of the One who already does.

Surrender is not giving up. It's giving in to gentleness, to mercy, to God, Himself. It's the quiet trust that what's breaking is also being reborn. Each tear that falls becomes holy water. Each ache, an offering. Each breath, a prayer that rises to Heaven and returns as peace.

Healing is not found in striving, but in yielding. It happens quietly, in the unseen places where your soul softens toward grace. It begins when you hand over your trembling heart to hands that have never failed you.

You are not being undone.

You are being re-shaped.

God is not rushing your recovery. He's restoring you piece by piece, memory by memory, until even the ruins begin to bloom.

This is the sacred rhythm of October. To let go. To be held. To be healed. Let this month become your altar of release, your sanctuary of surrender. Let the light reach every hidden place that aches to be free. Do not fear the stillness. Do not resist the softening. You are safe in the hands of the One who makes all things new. Trust the holy unfolding. Trust the quiet transformation.

Trust that in every letting go, something eternal is taking root.

October 1

Hi God, it's me.

A new month begins.

I can feel You inviting me
to loosen my grip again.

To breathe deeper. To trust more.
To surrender what I've been holding too tightly.

This month, I don't want to force or fight.

I want to flow with You.

Teach me that surrender
is not weakness but worship.

Not giving up.
But giving over.

This October is a holy offering of release.

Every thought. Every goal. Every plan.
Every piece of me returning to You.

Here I am, God.

Open.
Humble.
Surrendered.

Yours.

October 2

Hi God, it's me.

I can feel You mending me quietly.
Not all at once. But little by little.

Like light
finding its way through
cracks I once tried to hide.

Healing doesn't rush.

It listens.
It lingers.

It loves me where I am.

You're teaching me
healing isn't proof of strength.

It's the grace of being held
while I'm still becoming whole.

So today, I won't hurry my heart.

I'll let Your gentleness do
what time alone never could.

Thank You, God,
for touching what hurts with mercy,
for staying close until peace returns.

October 3

Hi God, it's me.

Some days,
surrender feels simple.

Other days,
it feels like standing
in the dark with open hands.

I keep wanting to know what's next,
while You ask me to rest in what is.

You remind me surrender is not silence.
It's a sacred conversation without words.

Surrender is trust spoken through stillness.

So today, I won't reach for control.

I'll reach for You instead.

I'll let Your will
be the rhythm of my day;
Your peace, the place I return to.

Hold me steady here, God.

In this quiet yielding,
in this holy pause
where my will
becomes
Yours.

October 4

Hi God, it's me.

I felt resistance rise in me today.

Not because I don't love You. But because obedience sometimes feels like sacrifice.

Like laying down
my timeline, my preferences,
my idea of how things should go.

You've never asked for perfection.

Just surrender.

You've never
led me into obedience
without filling it with purpose.

So soften me again, God.

Not just to say *yes*, but to mean it.

To walk in surrender.
To live it in every choice.
To trust You more than my comfort.

This is the path I choose again and again.

I surrender all to You.

October 5

Hi God, it's me.

I've been thinking about the
kind of life that pleases You.

Not the loudest.
Not the most accomplished.

But the one that keeps saying *yes*.

Yes when it's hard.
Yes when it's quiet.

Yes when no one else understands.

Let that be me.

The one who keeps going.
The one who doesn't give up.

The one who trusts surrender
always leads somewhere sacred.

Though I can't see it yet, I know
You're building something beautiful.

Teach me to yield without fear.
To bow my will without hesitation.
To lay everything down and call it holy.

God, keep my heart soft and surrendered,
until even my silence becomes a holy *yes*.

October 6

Hi God, it's me.

I didn't realize how much healing requires surrender.

To release what hurt me, I have to stop rehearsing it.
To be made new, I have to stop reaching back.

Some days, letting go feels like losing a part of me. But You remind me it's the only way to make room for peace.

You're teaching me
surrender and healing
walk hand in hand.

One softens the heart.
The other restores it.

So today, I lay down what still aches.

The memory.
The need to understand.
The story I kept trying to rewrite.

I trust You to make it mean something holy. To breathe over what's broken and bring beauty from what I release.

I don't need to fix it anymore.
I just need to give it back to You.

October 7

Hi God, it's me.

I'm learning surrender
isn't a single moment.

It's a daily returning.

A quiet *yes*
that keeps unfolding.

Each morning,
You invite me
to release again.

The plans, the pace, the worry,
the need to know how it all ends.

Some days my trust feels strong.
Other days my hands still shake.

Still, You're gentle with me.

You wait until my heart
remembers You are safe.

So today, I surrender again.

Not with fear.
But with faith.

Your way is always softer,
always surer, always love.

October 8

Hi God, it's me.

Obedience doesn't
always come naturally.

There are days I still want
to choose my own way.

The easier way.
The faster way.

The way that doesn't stretch me.

But every time I've trusted You,
You've led me somewhere better.

Somewhere deeper.

Somewhere more rooted in purpose than
anything I could have planned on my own.

Remind me of that today.

Following You is never a waste.
It's always the way back home.

October 9

Hi God, it's me.

Surrender is softer
than I thought it would be.

It doesn't shout.

It whispers.
It humbles.

It makes room for You.

It's the stillness after all my striving ends. The
peace that comes when I finally unclench my heart.

You meet me there.

Not asking for perfection.

Just permission.

Teach me to live with open hands, to release
what was never mine and trust what always was:

You.

And when I yield, dear God, let
Your presence fill the empty spaces.

Your breath moves through every quiet corner of my
soul, until what remains of me belongs entirely to You.

October 10

Hi God, it's me.

My heart feels heavy tonight. The
kind of ache that lingers in silence.

I keep trying to understand
why letting go hurts so much.

But maybe surrender was never meant to feel easy. Maybe
it's meant to make room for something only You can mend.

You see what I've laid down.

The love.
The hope.

The pieces of me still trembling in Your hands.

Gather them gently, God.

Breathe on what I've released.
Heal what I've placed before You.

Let every fragment find its way
back to wholeness in Your care.

All I have left is trust.

God, please let that be enough.

October 11

Hi God, it's me.

There's a quiet
peace after the breaking,
a softness I didn't expect.

Maybe this is what healing feels like.

Not sudden, but slow.
Not loud, but holy.

You're teaching me what
I surrender doesn't vanish.

It transforms.

You take what I release and
shape it into something new.

Something gentler.
Something true.

And though I still feel the ache, it no longer owns me.
Your presence fills the empty spaces it left behind.

Keep teaching me, dear God.
Healing isn't about forgetting.

It's about finding You in everything I've let go of.

October 12

Hi God, it's me.

I used to think healing meant going
back to who I was before the hurt,
before the breaking.

But You keep showing me
healing isn't about returning.

It's about becoming.

You're shaping me through every ache,
through every quiet mercy, through every
piece of peace that finds its way back to me.

I can feel it now.

The soft renewal, the holy
rebuilding of what once felt lost.

You're not restoring me to what was.
You're making me all brand new.

And this time, God,
I want to stay whole
in Your hands.

October 13

Hi God, it's me.

I'm learning surrender and
rest are the same language.

When I stop striving, I can finally hear You breathe.
When I stop reaching, I can finally feel Your peace.

Rest isn't idleness.
It's trust in motion.

It's the heart saying,
I don't have to hold it anymore.

You're already holding it all.

The plans.
The timing.

The pieces of me still unfolding.

My rest honors You.

My stillness worships Your name.

Let me stay here, God.

Quiet before You, anchored in grace,
breathing in the holiness of being still with You.

October 14

Hi God, it's me.

It's strange
how peace comes
after the hardest release.

Like quiet light spilling into
the space where pain once lived.

Maybe this is what surrender does.
It clears the room for You to enter.

I don't need to rebuild what
You've already redeemed.

I just need to rest where
Your will has settled.

You hold what I've laid down.
You heal what I no longer chase.

And here
in this stillness,
I finally understand.

Nothing
surrendered
to You is ever lost.

October 15

Hi God, it's me.

I said things I shouldn't have.
I let anger speak louder than love.

And now my heart feels heavy with what I can't take back.

I know this isn't who I want to be.
But it's who I was in that moment.

Defensive, hurt, trying to protect myself instead of reflecting You.

Dear God, please help me surrender
the part of me that wants to fight.
the pride that wants to be right,
the voice that rises to defend
instead of listen.

Teach me to lay down my anger before it hardens into bitterness. To let grace speak where ego once lived.

I don't want to win, God.
I want to be healed.

So take this anger. Take the need to prove.
Turn it into peace that restores instead of divides.

Make me gentle again, dear God.

When I'm right. When I'm hurt.
Even when it costs my pride.

October 16

Hi God, it's me.

I've been sitting with the
weight of my own words.

The ones I wish I could gather
back and place at Your feet.

I know You've already forgiven me.
But I still feel the ache of what I've broken.

Dear God, teach me to receive the grace You've already given.
To stop punishing myself for what You've already washed clean.

Let Your mercy move through the places where shame
still hides. Let Your love speak louder than my regret.

I don't want to live inside the moment I failed.

I want to live
inside the forgiveness
that found me there.

Thank You, God, for calling even this:

the humbling, the remorse,
the returning,
holy.

October 17

Hi God, it's me.

I've made peace with You. But not
everyone will make peace with me.

Some hearts take longer to heal.
Some wounds stay guarded.

I can't make anyone see my repentance or trust my change.

You're teaching me surrender also
means releasing how I'm received.

I can't control their healing.

Only my honesty, my softness, my willingness to love again.

So, I place it all in Your hands.

The silence, the distance,
the unfinished things.

If reconciliation is meant to bloom, let it be in Your timing.

Dear God, and if it never does,
let there still be peace in me.

I forgive them.
I release myself.

I rest in the grace of being understood by You.

October 18

Hi God, it's me.

I can feel You
working beneath the surface, touching
the parts of me that once reacted in pain.

You're showing me that healing
isn't just about what happened.

It's about who I'm becoming because of it.

You're softening
what was hardened,
quieting what was defensive.

Dear God, You're teaching my heart
how to choose peace before pride.

This is the kind of change I can't force.

Only You can create it,
holy from the inside out.

Keep shaping me, God.

Until my first response is love,
and my last word is always grace.

October 19

Hi God, it's me.

Forgiveness has settled in now.

Not like a shout,
but like a whisper
that lingers.

The heaviness has lifted,
and what's left is peace.

Not because everything is fixed.
But because my heart finally is.

Your mercy
met me where I fell apart,
and now I can breathe again:

softly, freely, whole.

I don't need to revisit what
You've already redeemed.

The wound is no longer the story.

Your grace is.

Thank You, God,
for the quiet after forgiveness,
for peace that feels like healing,
and for love that makes me new.

October 20

Hi God, it's me.

The storm has passed, but its
echoes still hum inside me.

Not loud.

Just faint reminders of where I've been.

And yet, the air feels lighter now.
The sky clearer. My soul unburdened.

Maybe that's what peace truly is.

Not the absence of storms
but the presence of You
after they end.

I see how You carried me through
what I thought would break me.

How even
in the wind and the weight,
You were whispering, *Be still.*

Now that it's quiet again,
Dear God, please teach me not to reach for the chaos.
Teach me to rest in the calm without fear of its ending.

This silence is holy. This stillness is the proof
I survived and was made softer in Your hands.

October 21

Hi God, it's me.

Peace has settled deeper now.

Not a feeling that comes and goes.
But a presence that moves with me.

It's in the way I breathe before I speak.

The way I pause before I react.

The way I walk through the day
fully aware that You are near.

This peace is sacred.

It's the proof of surrender taking root.

It's not silence.
It's communion.

It's not stillness.
It's trust embodied.

You're teaching me to live softly in a world that rushes; to carry Your calm like holy fire; to move as one who knows I'm held.

Let my steps be prayer.
Let my peace be praise.

My life is the quiet echo of Your presence within me.

October 22

Hi God, it's me.

Surrender changes everything.

It softens what fear once hardened.
It steadies what worry once swayed.

God, I used to think peace came from everything going right.
But now I see it blooms when I stop resisting what You allow.

Every time I release my grip,
You show me how strong and
faithful Your hands truly are.

You're teaching me surrender isn't giving up.

It's giving in to grace.

It's trusting the detours are holy ground.

Keep me in that posture, God.

Open in spirit.
Low before You.
Yielded in love.

For it's in surrender
that my soul finally rests.
And in resting, I find You again.

October 23

Hi God, it's me.

Trust feels tender right now.

It isn't loud or certain.

It's quiet work
soft and steady,
like You.

I don't have to know what
You're doing to believe it's good.

I just have to keep
showing up with
open hands.

Trust isn't just a feeling.
It's a way of breathing.

A way of living in rhythm with Your will.

When doubt whispers,
meet me with patience.

When fear returns,
wrap me in peace.

Keep teaching my heart the gentle work of trust:

to learn, to listen, to let You lead.

October 24

Hi God, it's me.

You've
taught me
how to let go.

Now,
You're teaching
me how to receive.

It's easier to release
than to open my hands again;
to let goodness find me after the ache.

I can feel You whispering,
This peace is for you too.
This love belongs here.

Healing has softened the ground,
and now Your grace can take root.

Dear God, help me not to shrink from
blessings or question why I'm worthy of it.

I welcome what You send with
quiet joy and unguarded faith.

I'm learning,
Lord, my God, that surrender
makes space for abundance.

Receiving is its own kind of worship.

October 25

Hi God, it's me.

Wholeness feels sacred, like a song
You've been writing in the quiet of my soul.

Not perfection.
But peace that breathes.

Soft. Steady. Sure.

The scars remain.
But they shine now.

Holy reminders of where grace entered.

You gathered what I scattered. You wove
together what I thought was beyond repair.

I'm not who I was before the breaking.

I'm something new.

Something touched by mercy.
Something held by You.

This is what healing truly is; the becoming
that happens when love does the mending.

Thank You, God, for making my brokenness
beautiful, and calling even my fragments holy.

October 26

Hi God, it's me.

Gratitude
keeps rising in me.

Not loud, but deep.

It hums beneath everything now.

A quiet awe for how You've carried me
through the unraveling, through the surrender,
through the slow sacred healing that changed me.

Every breath feels borrowed.
Every moment, a small miracle.

You've turned what once hurt into wisdom I can hold.
You've turned what once felt empty into space for grace.

I see You everywhere now.

In what left.
In what stayed.
In what became new.

I thank You, Holy One,
for the peace that follows surrender,
for the beauty that blooms after breaking,
and also for the love that never once let go.

October 27

Hi God, it's me.

I can feel the month slowing down, like
the hush that comes after a long exhale.

There's a gentleness here.

The kind that only comes
after release and repair.

I've laid down so much.

And in return,
You've given me peace.

Not all at once, but in pieces; like morning
light finding its way through broken clouds.

You've been patient with me,
teaching me how to let go
without losing myself.

How to heal without hardening.

Surrender wasn't the ending. It was
the sacred beginning of becoming whole.

Thank You, God, for staying close through every breaking
and mending; for teaching my heart how to rest in Yours.

October 28

Hi God, it's me.

I've been thinking about
how gentle Your healing
truly is.

It doesn't hurry the heart.
It doesn't push the process.

It simply waits until
I'm ready to be soft again.

Every time I surrender, You meet me there.
Quietly, faithfully, like light returning after rain.

You take the ache and turn it into peace.
You take what I release and breathe life into it.

Nothing I've laid down has been forgotten.
It's all been woven into something beautiful.

I can feel it now.

The strength that comes from trust.
The calm that comes from being held.

Surrender is sacred ground.
The healing is proof of Your love.

October 29

Hi God, it's me.

I've learned surrender is power,
though sometimes it looks like yielding.

It's the quiet strength of hands unclosed.
The moment pride dissolves and peace takes its place.
The holy exchange of control for communion.

You've shown me glory lives here.

In the letting go,
in the bowing low,
in the trust that follows release.

Every time I yield, heaven moves closer.
Every time I soften, Your Spirit fills the space.

This is where Your power dwells, God.

Not in striving.
But in surrender.

Not in holding on,
but in handing
everything
over to
You.

October 30

Hi God, it's me.

Surrender
has changed
the shape of me.

There's
a calm I didn't earn,
a peace I couldn't make.

You've taken
the tension from my grip
and filled it with grace instead.

You've turned striving into
stillness, and fear into faith.

Now I see,
the more I yield,
the more You reveal.

Every release becomes revelation.

The holy work of surrender:

to be emptied of myself
and filled with You.

Surrender makes my life
a living prayer of trust.

My heart rests open to Your will alone.

October 31

Hi God, it's me.

This month has been an altar.

Each surrender, a prayer.
Each tear, a baptism.

You've taken what I released
and turned it into peace.

You've taken
what I feared
and made it faith.

I see now healing wasn't a moment.

It was You
meeting me again
and again in the letting go.

Nothing was wasted.

Not the ache.
Not the waiting.

Not a single whispered *yes*.

I end this month emptied, open, and full of You.

NOVEMBER

Gratitude & Reflection

Gratitude is the language of remembrance. It draws you back to the quiet truth that God has been here all along; guiding, providing, carrying you through every season that felt too heavy to bear. This month invites you to pause and look around. To see how grace has been gathering in the details you once overlooked.

Thankfulness doesn't always rise from joy. Sometimes, it grows from survival. From realizing that even in the ache, you were never abandoned. Every answered prayer and every moment of silence have shaped the person you're becoming. Gratitude turns memory into worship. It transforms what happened into a hymn of praise.

Reflection is sacred work. It allows your spirit to gather meaning from the months behind you and strength for the ones to come. As you remember, do so gently. Honor where you've been without clinging to it. Let each memory become evidence of God's unfailing love, written quietly between the lines of your days.

So breathe slowly. Whisper thanks for the simple things. Let your heart rest in the knowing that you have been held through it all.

Gratitude is not just something you express. It's something you live. It becomes the way you see, the way you move, the way you love. It softens your words and steadies your steps. It reminds you that peace was never lost. It's always been waiting beneath the noise, in the stillness of trust.

This is the peace of November. To look back with thanks. To move forward with grace. And to dwell, even for a moment, in the holy awareness that every breath is a blessing. Every day is a gift still unfolding in God's hands.

November 1

Hi God, it's me.

It's a new month.

A new chance to notice
how much I already have.

I spend so much time asking for what's next
that I forget to honor what's already here.

Thank You for the blessings
I didn't even recognize as blessings.

The answered prayers
I stopped noticing.

The grace that
carried me quietly.

Open my eyes wider this month.

Let me become someone who
notices Your goodness everywhere.

Let my gratitude become
a prayer without words.

Let every breath I take
be a way of saying,
"I see You here."

November 2

Hi God, it's me.

Joy feels softer now.

Like sunlight through quiet leaves.
Like still water reflecting grace.

It doesn't shout anymore.

It hums.
It lingers.

It lives between moments I used to overlook.
It rises when I slow down enough to notice.

God, I remember how far You've brought me.
I whisper thanks for things I once rushed past.

Joy isn't something I have to find.
It's what grows when gratitude takes root.

When I pause to reflect, I see You everywhere.

In the quiet grace of an ordinary morning, in the warmth
of laughter, in the soft mercy of another chance.

Joy begins in remembrance that
gratitude opens the heart to feel You near.

Dear God, You're the reason
my soul can rest and still sing.

You are the joy beneath it all.

November 3

Hi God, it's me.

Today I'm choosing gratitude
even though everything isn't perfect.

It's never been about perfection.
It's always been about presence.

About seeing You
in the middle of it all.

The mess.
The beauty.

The slow, sacred becoming.

Thank You for never leaving me.

Dear God, I thank You
for the strength I didn't realize
You were building while I waited.

I'm not where I used to be
and that's worth celebrating.

Today, I celebrate the person I've become
through Your grace, Your mercy, Your love.

November 4

Hi God, it's me.

Gratitude changes
the way I see everything.

It softens my frustration.
It rewrites my complaints.

It helps me notice the way You're blessing
me in ways I didn't even think to ask for.

God, teach me to live thankfully.

Not just in big moments.
But in small, ordinary ones.

I want gratitude to be my habit.

My language.
My posture.

Dear God, gratitude is the rhythm of my days.
The quiet echo of love returning to its Source.

November 5

Hi God, it's me.

Sometimes, I forget joy
was woven into me from
the very beginning.

Before I ever asked for more,
You had already called me enough.

God, I spend so much time waiting for something
to arrive when the gift has always been within me.

The breath You gave, the heart You shaped,
the soul You made to mirror Your light.

Joy is not the proof of a perfect life.
It's the reflection of a grateful one.

It blooms
when I remember
being alive is a blessing.

Thank You, God, for crafting me with care. For filling
me with Your presence and calling that presence good.

I've learned through ancient wisdom
that You made me with divine intention.

Your love lives in me, joyful and eternal.

November 6

Hi God, it's me.

Sometimes, it overwhelms me.
The thought that I belong to You.

That the same hands that
shaped the stars also shaped me.

Your breath became my breath.
Your light chose to live inside my skin.

I carry divinity in a human frame, and the more
I remember that, the more I rise in Your light.

Dear God, to be
Your child is to walk
with holy inheritance.

To know that love is not something I chase.
But something that breathed me into being.

Father God, thank You
for reminding me who I am.

A reflection of eternity
wrapped in flesh and grace.

My life mirrors this truth:

every word, every act, every dream
bears witness to the wonder of being
Yours.

November 7

Hi God, it's me.

I am Yours.

And because I am,
my life carries intention.

You breathed vision into my being
and wove meaning through my days.

You didn't just create me.

You called me.

You placed light within my hands
and asked that I build with love.

Purpose isn't always loud.

Sometimes it whispers
through the ways I show kindness,
through the courage to begin again,
through the quiet choice to believe.

God, thank You for trusting me to reflect You here; and for shaping my steps to serve something greater than myself.

My work is worship.
My becoming is praise.
My life is gratitude in motion.

To serve You.

November 8

Hi God, it's me.

Because I am Yours,
I'm never without direction.

When the path feels hidden,
Your hand is steady on my soul.

You guide in ways I don't always see.
Through gentle nudges, divine delays,
and doors that open only in Your timing.

Every detour carries wisdom.
Every pause is protection.

You've never led me astray.

Only closer to who
I'm becoming in You.

Thank You, God, for being
both compass and companion.

Thank You, Father, for walking with me
through the unknown until peace finds me again.

Your guidance is a melody
my spirit learns by heart.

It hums through the quiet.
It moves through the dark.
It leads me home to You.

November 9

Hi God, it's me.

You are here,
woven through my being
like breath through silence.

Your nearness is not a feeling.

It's truth.
It's life itself.

You move through me
like peace that knows where to rest,
like wisdom that doesn't need words.

In every heartbeat, I sense Your rhythm.
In every pause, I find Your presence.

Dear God, thank You
for making Yourself known
in ways beyond understanding:

in stillness, in being, in me.

You are not found; for
You have never been lost.

You are simply here.

I give thanks to be this close to eternity.

November 10

Hi God, it's me.

You're still shaping me.

Not through rush or demand.
But through grace that unfolds slowly.

Each day,
something softens.
Something opens.

Something in me learns
to mirror more of You.

Becoming is sacred work.

It's patience and trust intertwined.

It's knowing growth isn't about
perfection, but about presence.

Thank You, God, for every season that refines me, for every moment that molds me closer to Your likeness.

I'm not who I was.
I'm not yet who I'll be.

I am Yours in every in-between.

Holy.

November 11

Hi God, it's me.

The more You shape me,
the more I feel Your love
reaching through my hands.

Service is no longer a task.
It's a thank You in motion.

A sacred echo of the
grace I've been given.

When I love,
You love through me.

When I give,
it's Your abundance
pouring outward.

This is how I worship.

Not only in prayer,
but in presence.

Not only in words, but also
in the way I show up for others.

God, thank You for allowing my life
to become a vessel of Your goodness.

Every kindness is communion. And every
act of care, a hymn that returns to You.

November 12

Hi God, it's me.

Peace is Your signature,
written gently across
the edges of my soul.

It comes when striving ends, when I finally
stop reaching and remember I'm already held.

Your peace is not a pause.

It's a presence.

It lives
beneath the noise,
waiting to be noticed.

I don't have to earn it.
I only have to rest in it.

Thank You, Father God, for the stillness
that finds me when my heart grows tired.

Thank You, Mother God, for the calm and
the warmth that reminds me You are near.

This quiet isn't empty.

It's holy.

The divine knowing that You're
keeping me safe in Your loving arms.

November 13

Hi God, it's me.

There's
a peace that settles
deeper than satisfaction.

A quiet joy
from knowing what You've given
is always more than enough.

I used to chase more.

More answers. More signs.
More proof of being seen.

I'm grateful
You've shown me contentment
isn't the absence of desire.

It's the fullness of trust.

It's standing still and finding
beauty in what already is.

Thank You, God, for teaching my heart to rest in the now.
For showing me gratitude multiplies whatever it touches.

This moment is sacred.
This breath is a gift.

I have everything I need because I have You.

November 14

Hi God, it's me.

You're never late.

You move in rhythms
that only heaven can hear.

Your timing is mercy protecting me from what's
not ready yet and preparing me for what is.

Every delay has purpose.

Every silence holds something
growing beneath the surface.

Dear God, thank You
for reminding me that
waiting is not wasting.

It's worship in slow motion.

I breathe between the seconds,
and trust what I can't yet see.

Your timing
is perfection dressed
in patience.

Dear God,
every season arrives
right on time in Your hands.

November 15

Hi God, it's me.

You have a way of mending
what I thought was beyond repair.

Not all at once.
Not through force.

But through love that works
in silence, patient and sure.

You heal in layers:

in forgiveness, in truth, in time.

What once felt broken now feels blessed.
What once ached with sorrow now beats with wisdom.

Thank You, God,
for touching the parts of me
that words could never reach.

I thank You for turning
pain into something sacred.

This is what grace is.

Not erasing the wound,
but letting it glow
in the light of
redemption.

November 16

Hi God, it's me.

When I look back, I see Your fingerprints on everything.
Even the places I once mistook for a lingering absence.

You were there in every beginning,
every breaking, every becoming.

The joy and the ache were both
invitations to know You deeper.

God, thank You for mercy that met me in motion.

Thank You for grace that waited when I wandered, and for
divine beauty that kept blooming even in the in-between.

Nothing has been wasted.
Every step has carried revelation.

This road is holy because You walk every step with me.
I can't see where it leads. But my heart knows the truth.

The destination is always You.

November 17

Hi God, it's me.

Through every season,
You've remained steady
when I stumbled.

Present when I wandered.
Kind when I forgot myself.

Your faithfulness has been the quiet rhythm beneath all the noises of the world, the steady flame that never burned out.

When I couldn't see the way, You were already there. Preparing paths, holding time, keeping promises I didn't know to pray for.

God,
thank You for never changing
in a world that always does.

I thank You for being
the same Love that carried me
yesterday, and will carry me still.

You are my constant.

My covenant.
My forever *Yes*.

My heart,
full of gratitude, bows to the One
who has never failed to be faithful.

November 18

Hi God, it's me.

Everything begins with Your love.

Every sunrise. Every heartbeat.
Every breath of grace is born from it.

Your love has carried me through what I didn't understand,
through seasons that stretched my soul and still called me home.

It's the melody beneath my prayers.
The calm that gathers around my name.

Thank You, God, for loving me completely.
Not for what I do, but for who I am to You.

Your love is the language
my spirit speaks fluently.

The endless echo
of where I come from,
and where I will always return.

November 19

Hi God, it's me.

The
world You made
is a living prayer.

The trees reach for heaven without hesitation.
The oceans keep rhythm with Your breath.
The sky stretches wide with endless faith.

Every part of creation
reminds me who You are.

Steady, vast.

Overflowing with beauty and order.

Mighty Creator,
thank You for painting
glory into everything.

Holiness is not confined to walls or words.

It lives in sunlight on still water.
In wind that carries whispers.
In soil that remembers rain.

All of it sings of You.

What a blessing to let my lips become
a sacred hymn that joins Your song.

November 20

Hi God, it's me.

You are everywhere.

In the soft hum of morning light,
in the laughter that drifts through open windows,
in the warmth of a hand reaching for mine.

It's easy to praise You
in the grand and glorious.

But today, I thank You
for the simple things.

The still moments. The quiet kindnesses.
The daily grace that holds me together.

Every small thing is a reminder
heaven touches earth in ways
I might miss if I move too fast.

Dear God, I thank You for the beauty
that doesn't need to announce itself.

I give thanks
for the holiness
woven into the ordinary.

You are here, in every gentle detail.

A lifetime of praise.

November 21

Hi God, it's me.

There's a stillness that speaks louder than words;
a sacred calm that wraps itself around my soul
and reminds me I'm never apart from You.

Your presence isn't something I enter.

It's where I already am.

It breathes through me, moves with me, lives
in every heartbeat that remembers its Source.

God, thank You for being here.

Not as a visitor, but as home.

There's nothing to ask for.

Nothing to fix.
Nothing to prove.

Only
this moment,
holy and whole,
held entirely in You.

In this stillness, I finally understand.

This is what love feels like
when it no longer needs a name.

November 22

Hi God, it's me.

Rest is trust.

The kind
that doesn't rush to understand,
but leans softly in Your keeping.

You never asked me to carry everything alone.
You only asked me to breathe, to believe, to be still.

Holy God, thank You
for peace that settles when I stop
striving and simply return to You.

In rest, I remember:

Your hands never tire.
Your heart never sleeps.

Here, in Your rest, I am whole.

November 23

Hi God, it's me.

Grace
is the breath that meets me
when I run out of words.

It finds me in every place I thought I'd failed You, and
transforms my shame into something soft and seen.

You never measure
me by what I've done.

But by who I am in You.

God, I thank You for divine mercy,
for every morning that begins again.

Your grace is not fragile.

It doesn't fade when I falter.

It gathers me.
It restores me.

It calls me beloved before
I even know how to answer.

This is love without conditions.
This is redemption that stays.

God, this is You.

November 24

Hi God, it's me.

There's a peace that comes
from knowing I belong to You.

Not because I earned it.
But because You desired it.

You wanted me
even when I wandered,
even when I forgot my name.

Your love has never
once lost sight of me.

It found me.

In the far places,
in the hidden places,
and led me home every time.

Mighty Supreme Creator God,
thank You for the comfort of being claimed, for the safety of being known, for the grace of being loved exactly as I am.

I'm not a visitor in Your heart.

I'm family.

Forever.

November 25

Hi God, it's me.

Some days, gratitude
begins with remembering.

When I look back,
I see the map of Your mercy.

The prayers You answered gently, the doors You closed in love, the moments You carried me when I thought I was walking alone.

Memory
becomes a sanctuary
where faith grows stronger.

Every recollection
is a testimony of grace.

Dear God, I give thanks for the stories written in stillness.
For the glimpses of Your hand woven through my history.

Holy One, the hard chapters
glow differently in hindsight.

They were never empty.
They were evidence of You.

I worship You, Holy God.

Every mercy is a promise kept.
A divine reminder You're faithful.

November 26

Hi God, it's me.

The month begins to close,
and my heart grows still.

Surrender no longer feels
like release, but like reverence.

It's the gentle bow
of my spirit to the
rhythm of Yours.

Peace is found not in what I hold,
but in what I place back in Your hands.

As the days turn
and the year leans forward,
I rest here in sacred alignment.

Faithful God,
I rest in quiet trust,
in love that carries me
exactly where You will.

November 27

Hi God, it's me.

Joy
has found me again,
morning light singing
to my heart and soul.

It lives
in the small moments,
in laughter that lingers,
in peace that hums softly
beneath the day.

God, thank You for reminding me
that joy isn't something to chase.

It's what blooms
when the soul is at rest and
when gratitude becomes breath.

As this month begins to fade,
I feel Your goodness everywhere:

alive in my heart, alive in the quiet,
alive in the joy of simply being Yours.

November 28

Hi God, it's me.

Thank You for the hearts You've
woven into the fabric of my life.

Family is love appointed.

A circle of souls chosen by Your
wisdom and kept by Your grace.

In their laughter,
I hear echoes of heaven.

In their presence,
I feel Your tenderness made real.

God, thank You for every soul
who has held me in prayer.

I'm grateful
for every hand
that has lifted mine.

Love flows through
us as Your breath.

A living reminder
that we were never
meant to walk alone.

When I count my blessings, God, my family's
names are among the holiest ones I speak.

November 29

Hi God, it's me.

Faith has carried me through every season.
Quietly, patiently, like light that refuses to fade.

It has been my anchor
when answers were hidden,
my song when silence stayed too long.

Thank You for the strength to believe beyond what I
see; for trust that grows deeper each time I let go.

Faith is not fragile.

It's fire and devotion.

A steady flame
that keeps burning
even when the wind comes.

God, as this month draws near its end,
I see how belief has shaped my becoming.

It's not something I hold.
It's something that holds me.

Belief in You.

November 30

Hi God, it's me.

Before this month folds into
memory, I pause in stillness.

Not to ask, but to adore.

You are
the beginning
and the becoming.

The breath within the breath. The light
that lingers after every sunset of my soul.

Thank You, Holy One,
for being more than what I seek.

For being Presence itself:
unchanging, unshaken, ever near.

God, You are mercy wrapped in mystery, love
without condition, holiness clothed in tenderness.

Every grace I've known was a glimpse of You.
Every moment of peace, a shadow of Your nearness.

I close this month in reverent *awe*.
Hands open, heart bowed, spirit full.

God, You are my dwelling place,
my constant, my eternal Amen.

DECEMBER

Return To Worship

Before the year closes its final page, there is a quiet call to return. Not to what was, but to Who has always been. December arrives like a sanctuary. A soft light after the storm. A gentle doorway for the weary and the wandering. A place for the soul to kneel and breathe again. It's the holy hush before new beginnings, the stillness where presence feels near and time itself feels tender, as if heaven leans a little closer to listen.

This month is not about doing.

It's about remembering.

Remembering where your strength came from. Remembering the One who held you together when life felt too heavy to carry. Remembering the God who walked with you through every season, even the ones you didn't speak about.

December is about laying every burden at God's feet. The striving, the questions, the triumphs, and the tears. All of it belongs in His hands. And in that sacred exchange, you find rest in the One who carried it all.

Worship becomes the language of release, the sacred rhythm of returning home. It's the soft confession of surrender. The whispered song that says, You were good then. You are good now. You will be good still. Worship is not simply sung with the mouth. It's breathed through the heart. It's lived through the posture of yielding, trusting, remembering, and returning.

Look back, and you will see God's fingerprints on every chapter. The laughter that lifted you. The loss that humbled you. The lessons that shaped you. The prayers that held you together when nothing else made sense. Nothing was wasted. Every moment became part of a hymn you didn't know you were singing.

God was there in the unraveling and the becoming, steady as light, faithful as breath. And He is here still, waiting in the quiet glow of December, whispering, *Come closer. Let Me show you how I've been loving you all along.*

Lift your eyes. Lift your hands. Lift your soul.

Every breath is a prayer. Every heartbeat, a hallelujah.

Your life becomes an altar where gratitude rises like incense and surrender feels like peace. The year may be ending, but the worship is eternal as God is. And as you step into the final days of this year, may your spirit remember: returning to God is never a step backward, but a homecoming of the soul.

December 1

Hi God, it's me.

I've come back to the quiet.

Back to the space where words are
worship and breath becomes prayer.

I wandered through so many days
trying to hold everything together.

But the truth is, I only find peace
when I'm face to face with You.

This month,
I don't want to perform,
and I don't want to strive.

God, I want to sit in Your presence
and remember what holy feels like.

Worship isn't always a song.
Sometimes, it's surrender.

It's the posture of my soul bowing low
to recognize the love that never left.

Dear God, gather all the pieces of me that grew
tired from trying. Let Your hands be my home again.

I'm here, God.

Ready to rest. Ready to listen. Ready to worship.

December 2

Hi God, it's me.

Glory
meets me
in the quiet.

In still air.
In soft light.

In the breath
that remembers You.

You were never far.

Just waiting for me to
slow down enough to see.

Worship rises not from
striving, but from *awe*.

Every
whisper of creation
echoes Your name.

And here I am:

small, still,
and full of wonder.

You are holy, God.

This moment is Yours.

December 3

Hi God, it's me.

Something
in me has softened.

The walls I built to stay
strong are beginning
to kneel.

I used to think worship
was lifting my hands high.

But now I know it's
the heart that bows first.

Every surrender becomes a song.
Every yielding becomes praise.

Take what I've held too tightly, God.
Take what was never mine to carry.

My heart bends toward You again.

This is my worship.
This is my *yes*.

December 4

Hi God, it's me.

Your light
finds me gently.

Not in thunder.
But in tenderness.

It slips through the cracks
of all I thought was ruined
and makes it radiant again.

You turn
the remnants
into reflection.

The ashes into awe.

What was broken
now glows with
grace.

You are the Light, God.
Within You, I am found.

December 5

Hi God, it's me.

Stillness is worship.

It's the quiet rising
of my soul toward You.

The breath between words
where heaven feels near.

In this calm, I'm reminded
Your presence doesn't rush.

It rests.

Peace becomes prayer.
Silence becomes song.

God, I need nothing else
but the nearness of You.

Here,
in the sacred hush,
my spirit kneels unseen,
and all creations whisper:

holy, holy, holy.

December 6

Hi God, it's me.

Gratitude
has a sound.

A melody only
love can hear.

It hums beneath the breath.
It trembles through the heart.
It fills the soul like morning light.

Every mercy
becomes a note of praise.
Every memory, a verse of grace.

You've been faithful in the silence and the storm.
I've seen Your goodness woven through it all.

My life sings softly back to You.

Every thank You, a hallelujah.
Every breath, a song of worship.

December 7

Hi God, it's me.

You've built
an altar within me.

Not of stone, but of spirit.
Not in a temple, but in my heart.

Every breath burns like incense.
Every act of love becomes offering.

You dwell here,
in the quiet chambers
of my becoming.

I am Yours.

Not just in song.
But in essence.

God, my life is a living sanctuary,
where all I am bows to all You are.

December 8

Hi God, it's me.

To
dwell with You
is to be home.

Not the kind built by hands.
But the kind the soul remembers.

God, every time I rest in You,
the ache in me turns into peace.

You're the stillness
beneath every storm;
the warmth that welcomes
what once was wandering.

I could search the world and never find
a place more holy than Your presence.

I'm here, God.

In the hush of Your nearness,
where love breathes first and
everything becomes light.

My spirit is folded in Your glory.
My heart kneels in unending *awe*.

Here, in You, Heaven is near.

December 9

Hi God, it's me.

Your glory
doesn't always
arrive with noise.

Sometimes,
it comes clothed in gentleness,
the light that touches morning leaves,
the peace that hums beneath my breath.

God, You are not
only in the heavens.

You are here, woven
into every quiet wonder.

The way the sun
warms my face.

The way grace finds me
without asking for perfection.

Majesty wears mercy so well.
Holiness feels like softness now.

In this still moment, I see You,
shining through everything
that yields to love.

December 10

Hi God, it's me.

Your presence moves
quietly through my day.

In the shimmer of
sunlight on the floor.

In the hum of dishes drying.

In the laughter that lingers
long after sound has faded.

God,
nothing is common
when You are near.

Every breath, every gesture,
carries the weight of heaven.

The smallest moments become
sacred when touched by love.

You are here, God,
turning the ordinary
into *awe*.

December 11

Hi God, it's me.

Joy is worship.

It rises, not from what's perfect,
but from what's been redeemed.

The way light returns after rain.

The way laughter finds me
even with tears still drying.

You are the source of every gladness.
The giver of every gentle delight.

This joy belongs to You, God.

Not loud, but pure.

A radiant hallelujah, spilling like
golden light across the altar of my heart.

It shimmers upward,
a song without sound,
declaring through every breath:

glory to the Holy One,
the God who makes all things new.

December 12

Hi God, it's me.

Faith
is the flame
that never dies.

When the wind rises,
when the night feels long,
it flickers with a holy defiance,
a whisper of trust that refuses to fade.

You breathe upon it,
and it glows again.

Not brighter.
But deeper.

Steady. Certain. Sure.

It's
the fire that warms my worship.
The light that leads me home.

And
even in darkness,
I see You there.

You're the Eternal Spark,
burning within my soul.

December 13

Hi God, it's me.

Belonging to You is not a place.

It's a presence.

It's the hush between heartbeats
where eternity breathes my name.

I'm not outside of You.
God, I'm within You.

Woven
through mercy,
anchored in grace.

You are the pulse beneath my being.
The endless *yes* beneath my soul.

In this holy union,
nothing is missing,
nothing is separate.

You are the sound.
I am the echo.

You are the fire.
I am the flame.

This, God!

This oneness is worship.

December 14

Hi God, it's me.

Grace has crowned this year.

Not because I earned it,
but because You are mercy
wearing time like a garment.

Every moment I thought was loss was
really love, bending low to lift me higher.

You gathered my fragments
and wove them into glory.

You turned my striving into song.

God, every chapter
of my life glimmers with
the shimmer of Your kindness.

You've been
the beginning
and the becoming.

The constant light at every turn.

I bow in *awe*, God,
beneath the crown of grace
You placed upon my days.

December 15

Hi God, it's me.

The days are quieting now.
The year is folding into Your hands.

What's left undone no longer feels heavy.
You will finish what was meant to be.

I lay it all before You.

Every triumph, every tear,
like petals returning to the
soil that grew them.

Nothing is wasted.
Nothing is lost.

You hold it all, God.

The start, the stumble,
the sacred in-between.

As this
season settles,
so does my soul.

Holy One, the closing is gentle,
because every fading moment
still carries the sound of You.

December 16

Hi God, it's me.

Time moves like a river.
You're the current beneath it.

Every moment:

the rushing,
the waiting,
the still.

They all flow through Your
hands untouched by hurry.

You were there when beginnings bloomed.
You're here now as endings turn to light.

The clocks may turn,
but Your love does not.

You write eternity
into passing days.

Nothing holy ever fades.

All things rest, but nothing is gone;
for every hour is held within the hands of God.

December 17

Hi God, it's me.

Becoming has been a sacred unveiling.

You've gathered me from my own
undoing, and called it creation.

Every breaking was a doorway to light.
Every silence a sanctuary for grace.

I see so clearly now.

You were never asking me to be more.
You were asking me to be *Yours*.

Through surrender, You shaped the unseen parts,
etching Your reflection into the soft clay of my soul.

Nothing was wasted.

Not a tear.
Not a trial.

Not a trembling *yes*.

You've written holiness into my becoming.
And here I stand, not finished, but full.

A living
testament to the One
who made me whole.

December 18

Hi God, it's me.

Silence is worship.

It holds
what words
cannot reach.

In the quiet,
my spirit kneels unseen,
touched by the nearness of You.

No asking.
No striving.

Only *awe*.

Here,
Your presence lingers
like light upon still water.

Here, the unseen becomes eternal.
And in this hush, I am wholly Yours.

A soul at rest within
the breath of God.

December 19

Hi God, it's me.

Amen
isn't an ending.

It's an echo.

The sound of forever
breathing through my soul.

You are
the first light
and the last flame.

The silence
between heartbeats,
the glory that never fades.

Every hallelujah finds its home in You.
Every breath returns to praise You.

Time may close its pages,
but worship does not cease.

It rises, unbound, unchanging.

The eternal Amen
to the everlasting
God.

December 20

Hi God, it's me.

Your light does not visit.

It abides.

It hums beneath my skin,
soft as dawn, sure as breath.

It moves through me like
mercy remembering its Source.

I'm no
longer searching
for where You are.

I'm learning how to see.

This light is holy.

It sanctifies
the ordinary, sets fire to the shadows,
turns my soul into a living sanctuary.

You are here, God.
Radiant and near.

The light within me is the life of You.

December 21

Hi God, it's me.

My heart
is Bethlehem.

Humble, waiting,
wide enough for wonder.

There's room here
for You to be born again.

In the silence, in the surrender,
in the spaces I once called empty.

You arrive quietly,
wrapped in light,
resting inside my *yes*.

No grand procession.
Just presence.

And in this tender light,
I feel heaven lean close.

The miracle was never distant.
It has always been within.

December 22

Hi God, it's me.

Morning is a miracle.

The kind
that doesn't shout,
but whispers:

I am making all things new.

You paint light over what was weary,
turning darkness into gentle revelation.

Every dawn feels like forgiveness.
Every ray, a reminder of resurrection.

You are
the warmth beneath the waiting,
the promise that never grows old.

As
the day begins, so does my worship.
Born again with the morning light.

December 23

Hi God, it's me.

Your nearness is the gift beyond gifts.
Closer than breath, truer than time.

You don't visit.
You dwell.

You don't knock.
You live within.

Every heartbeat is an altar.

Every
inhale a meeting place
of heaven and earth.

There is no distance left to cross.

Only presence to behold.

In this sacred closeness, time bows low,
eternity breathes, and my soul whispers:

Emmanuel.

God with us.
God within me.

December 24

Hi God, it's me.

Night
has never
felt so holy.

The earth is hushed,
and heaven leans near.

The air glows
with unseen glory,
as if creation itself
is holding its breath.

Love has entered the world again.
Quietly, completely, wrapped in light.

Every shadow bows to wonder.
Every heart awakens to grace.

This is the night
the world remembers
how close You've always been.

And here,
beneath this holy light,
my soul kneels.

In awe. In worship. In love.

December 25

Hi God, it's me.

Glory has dawned.

The Light
the prophets longed for now burns
in every heart that dares to believe.

Heaven
has touched the earth,
and nothing is the same.

You have come,
not as thunder,
but as tenderness.

Love made visible.
Hope made human.

Every heart has become
the cradle of Your presence.

This is holy morning.
This is sacred birth.

Christ within us,
the everlasting
Hallelujah.

December 26

Hi God, it's me.

The world
is quieter today,
but the light remains.

It shimmers softly in the corners of ordinary life.
In kindness exchanged, in laughter reborn,
in peace that feels like breath.

Your glory
didn't leave
with the morning.

It stayed.
It stays.

You are not a moment.

You're
the meaning
behind them all.

As the day unfolds, I carry
the afterglow of heaven.

Gentle. Steady. Near.

Love has come.
Love remains.

December 27

Hi God, it's me.

Your story did not end in the manger.

That wooden cradle; rough, unpolished, meant for feeding animals became a throne for heaven.

Straw cradled glory.
Silence held salvation.

What was ordinary was made
holy because You were there.

It keeps unfolding still.

In every act of grace,
in every heart that loves,
in every soul that listens.

Your presence
moves like breath through time,
still creating, still calling, still here.

The manger was never just a place.

It was a promise that You choose the lowly, the overlooked, the simple, to reveal Yourself again.

As I walk through these ordinary days, I hear it.

The whisper of forever woven into now.

December 28

Hi God, it's me.

The days after carry
their own kind of glory.

Not loud, not shining with celebration.
But tender, like embers after flame.

The miracle
moves quietly, faithfully, authentically,
through the gentle rhythms of living.

In eyes that soften with understanding.
In hands that give without asking.
In hearts that choose love again.

You are here
in the quiet return of life itself,
turning it holy with Your touch.

The light
of Bethlehem burns on
not above me, but within.

The wonder
remains, God.

So does my worship.

December 29

Hi God, it's me.

Wonder
still rests on everything.

It hums beneath the hush,
a sacred weight too holy for words.

You've filled the year with unseen mercies.
You filled it with threads of grace woven
through moments I almost missed.

And now,
as time begins to close its hands,
I feel the heaviness of beauty.

How even endings can be full of You.

Every breath
feels borrowed from heaven.
Every heartbeat a quiet thank You.

You've been faithful, God.
From first light to final glow.

December 30

Hi God, it's me.

The year is bowing low.

And so am I.

Every joy, every sorrow, every sacred in-between
return to You now offered, whole, complete.

Time
has been a teacher and a testament,
whispering through every moment:

You were here.

And You were, God.

In the breaking and the blooming.
In the silence and the song.

I release what was,
and bless what will be.

This closing is my benediction.
A final amen wrapped in gratitude.

Holy One, the year may end.
Your faithfulness never will.

December 31

Hi God, it's me.

The last light of the year
leans softly across the sky.

And I stand here in the glow
of everything You've done.

What a journey it has been.

Held, stretched, refined,
yet never abandoned.

You were
the constant in all my becoming.
The still voice beneath every storm.

I have nothing left to offer but *awe*.

The days have spoken their stories,
and each one ends in Your name.

So I whisper it now, God,
not as farewell, but as forever.

Amen.

The last word of time.
The first word of eternity.

A Prayer Of Completion

Hi God, it's me.

We've reached the final page.

But not the end.

Every word, every pause, every tear
that touched the lines were Yours.

You whispered, and I followed.
You guided, and I wrote.

What began as prayer became presence.
What began as longing became love.

I offer this work back to You;
every sentence, every silence,
every soul it will touch.

Dear God, let it carry Your light where mine cannot reach.
Let it heal, let it transform, long after I've finished writing.

This is not goodbye, God.

It's gratitude.
It's reverence.
It's *awe*.

God, I thank You for writing with me,
for being the story within the story.

Amen.

A Benediction For The Soul

You've journeyed through a year of sacred dialogue. Through trust and surrender, joy and stillness, healing and hope. And through it all, God has been whispering, reminding you that He was never far. Every prayer you whispered, was a love letter exchanged between heaven and your heart. You have not simply read these words. You have *lived* them. You have prayed them into being.

Carry this truth with you. God is not just the beginning of your story. He is every moment in between. He is presence, promise, and peace all at once. When the next chapter of your life unfolds, may you return to this quiet knowing: that you can always begin again. That every breath can be prayer. And that these conversations with God, your conversations with Him, never truly ends.

God is always with you, speaking and listening.

Go in light. Go in love. Go with God.

You are loved.

A Note From The Author

Thank you for journeying with me through this sacred year of conversations. Every page you turned and every prayer you whispered became a meeting place between your heart and heaven. This book was never meant to be just a collection of words. It was meant to be an invitation to listen, to breathe, and to remember that God has always been near.

As a writer, my favorite person to write to is God.

Even when I am not writing, the One I trust most to speak with throughout the day and night is Him. My conversations with God keep me aligned, centered, and awake to His presence. They remind me that I am safe, I am known, I am seen, and I am loved. They draw me back to peace when I wander and restore my faith when I forget who I am.

These pages are an offering of that love. Each reflection was written from a place of communion, where silence became language and prayer became poetry. I pray that as you close this book, you open your own heart to the ongoing conversation God is already having with you.

May you never doubt that He hears you. May you never question that He is with you. And may you always find your way back to His presence, where every breath becomes prayer and every moment becomes grace.

With love and gratitude,

C P Beauvoir

LEEF PUBLISHING
THE STORIES OF OUR HEARTS

www.ingramcontent.com/pod-product-compliance
Lightning Source LLC
Chambersburg PA
CBHW071733150426
43191CB00010B/1556